AF715224

Start Investing in Stocks

Start Investing in Stocks

Your complete beginner's guide to buying shares and building long-term wealth

Julian Crest

Mindful Pages

Published in 2025

ISBN: 9789371774185 (PB)
ISBN: 9789371776325 (eBook)

Published by

Mindful Pages
Imprint of Alpha Editions LLC
312 W. 2nd St #1834
Casper, WY 82601, USA

All rights reserved.
No part of this publication may be reproduced, distributed, or transmitted in any form or by any means — including photocopying, recording, or other electronic or mechanical methods — without the prior written permission of the publisher, except in the case of brief quotations used in reviews or permitted by applicable copyright law.
This book was developed using advanced writing tools to support the drafting and ideation process. All content has been thoughtfully curated, refined, and reviewed to ensure quality and relevance.

Content

Introduction
Ownership as a Way of Seeing

At some quiet, often unremarkable moment, nearly all of us confront a question that refuses to leave: Am I truly building something, or simply surviving? It rarely arrives in a philosophical form. Instead, it whispers through the background hum of daily transactions, the subtle unease of seeing prices outpace salaries, or in the late-night scroll through "how to invest" guides that open a bewildering tangle of charts, jargon, and conflicting counsel.

This book begins before any of that. It begins not with the mechanics of buying a stock, but with the more fundamental question: why would you want to own one at all? Not just one, but many—over time, with attention, with intention.

For all its complexity, the stock market is, at heart, a mechanism for ownership. Yet most of us have been conditioned to treat it as a game, a gamble, a spectacle. We speak of "winning" and "losing" as if it were sport rather than one of the most potent engines of long-term human progress. We are encouraged to chase trends, time entries, exit quickly, follow the "smart money." Rarely, however, are we invited to view the market as a space where agency and identity converge—a place to practise stewardship rather than speculation.

That perspective is what this book seeks to cultivate.

To invest is, in a sense, an act of faith. Not in blind optimism or in the certainty of growth, but in your capacity to make considered decisions amidst uncertainty, and to trust time—not tactics—to bear the weight of returns. At the core of intelligent investing is ownership. And that word—ownership—is deceptively simple. Here, it signifies more than holding assets; it is a claim on decisions, narratives, and a long-term vision.

It begins with seeing differently. You are not buying a ticker symbol; you are not reacting to headlines, emulating strategies, or hoping a clever move will liberate you from work. You are choosing to participate in the real economy, to support businesses that solve problems, generate value, and endure. You are becoming a stakeholder in stories measured not by daily fluctuations, but by the quiet compounding of thoughtful decisions.

Reframing investing as identity rather than mere activity is essential. Without this perspective, no technical skill can fortify you against turbulence or short-term noise. Once internalised, however, the act of investing shifts: it ceases to be a bet and becomes a practice.

And like any practice worth pursuing—be it writing, parenting, or leadership—mastery does not arrive overnight. It demands discipline, curiosity, patience, and, above all, self-awareness.

This book begins there: with you. Why do you wish to invest? Which narratives—cultural, familial, generational—shape your ideas of money, risk, and success? What fears tether your decisions? What assumptions quietly steer your actions? Before brokerages, balance sheets, or portfolio allocations, we must first explore the internal landscape. The most significant variable in your investing journey is not the stock you select, but how you think, react, and decide—habits that can be understood, strengthened, and refined.

Structured as a companion for this evolution, the book assumes no prior expertise while respecting intelligence. It avoids overwhelming jargon or abstract theory, offering instead clear frameworks—mental models, behavioural tools, psychological insights—designed to cultivate a resilient, enduring investing practice. Not merely to buy shares, but to become someone who invests with clarity and composure.

The chapters that follow examine technical, emotional, and philosophical dimensions of investing, grounded firmly in reality. Stocks are presented not as abstractions, but as extensions of living businesses. Markets are interpreted not only through earnings and macro data, but through human psychology. You will learn to cultivate calm amid volatility, nurture a long-term mindset, and develop discernment: knowing when to act, and when patience serves best.

Throughout, you are invited to embrace a central principle: ownership shapes perspective. Holding a business—even a fraction of one—alters how you view work, leadership, innovation, and sustainability. It transforms wealth from mere accumulation into participation, from extraction into contribution.

This is no romantic notion. Ownership has historically wielded immense power, shaping behaviours, sustaining families, building institutions, and transferring values across generations. To own is to accept responsibility, and in that responsibility, investing becomes profoundly personal.

Whether you are choosing your first stock or your fiftieth, the objective is clarity over speed, wealth as a tool rather than a trophy. The aim is to build freedom, security, generosity, and legacy. This book encourages thinking in decades while acting in decisive moments, learning deeply yet deciding simply, pursuing growth while defining sufficiency.

Practical guidance—opening brokerage accounts, identifying worthwhile businesses, managing emotional swings—is interwoven with reflective exercises: drafting a personal investment manifesto, assessing risk tolerance, establishing rituals to stabilise your mind. Each chapter pairs insight with action, recognising that understanding alone is insufficient.

This is not a guide to beating the market. The market is not an adversary; it is an environment. As a sailor learns to navigate the wind rather than control it, so must the investor adapt, observe, and act with composure, respecting the forces around them.

Investing, then, becomes a mirror of self-knowledge. Market volatility often reflects internal volatility. To learn investing is to learn oneself: recognising when fear drives action, when fantasy or avoidance dictates choices, and gradually replacing impulsive habits with measured, intentional ones.

Wealth is never only what you accumulate; it is what you carry: perspective, confidence, stewardship, time. It grants the ability to decide from strength rather than desperation. Money is a component of this, not its totality.

If you seek a list of "hot stocks" or a magic formula for instant gains, you may find disappointment. But if your aim is to build something enduring—to own purposefully, to grow patiently, to invest with meaning—you are in the right place.

Let us begin, then, not by asking what to buy, but by asking: what kind of investor do you wish to become?

That question will guide every decision that follows.

Chapter 1
The Stock Market Isn't a Casino—It's a Mirror

There is a quietly pervasive metaphor in popular culture that casts the stock market as a kind of roulette wheel: glamorous, risky, and fundamentally capricious. It is a story constructed less from lived experience than from spectacle. Films dramatise shouting traders, tumbling tickers, fortunes made and lost in minutes. Anecdotes at dinner tables recount cousins who "made a killing" or neighbours who "lost everything." Absent direct engagement, many internalise this mythology as truth: the market is a casino, and investing is an act of blind chance.

But metaphors shape perception, and perception shapes behaviour. If you approach the stock market as a casino, your actions will follow suit. You will chase thrills instead of strategy, mistake noise for signal, and equate movement with meaning. You may ride waves of euphoria only to retreat in fear, never fully grasping the underlying dynamics. You may linger on the sidelines, convinced that investing is not for people like you—perhaps raised to prize prudence over risk, stability over volatility. Or worse, you may treat the market as a theatre for fantasies, hoping for a quick win rather than cultivating ownership.

This chapter dismantles that metaphor and proposes a more grounded, empowered perspective. The stock market is not a casino. It is not a rigged machine designed to punish the inexperienced or reward the aggressive. Rather, it is a mirror: reflecting not only economic fundamentals, but the psychology of the collective—hopes, fears, biases, and beliefs—interacting within a fluid system of valuation. To navigate it intelligently, you must first examine the narratives you have inherited about money, risk, and what investing actually entails.

These narratives often originate in childhood. Perhaps you grew up in a household where money was scarce, or abundant but unspoken.

Perhaps the stock market was framed as dangerous, reserved for experts, or fundamentally dishonest. Perhaps you were taught investing is for "other people"—those with inside knowledge, excess capital, or a tolerance for gambling. These inherited beliefs are far from neutral; they embed themselves into your financial identity and subtly guide your choices until you interrogate them.

Consider the archetype of the "get-rich-quick" investor. This figure looms large in financial folklore: someone who spotted a hot stock early, bought low, and cashed out at the right moment. It is seductive but misleading. For every such story, there are countless quiet failures—people who chased trends, abandoned principles, and were left with regret. Yet these tales rarely circulate. As with all mythologies, survivorship bias distorts the cultural lens, glorifying speculation while marginalising patience, research, and true ownership.

Returning to first principles provides clarity. What is a share, fundamentally? Not a flickering symbol on a screen, not a graph line, not a lottery ticket. A share represents a legal claim on a portion of a real company. When you buy stock, you are not gambling on a number—you are becoming a co-owner of a business with employees, customers, strategies, risks, and cash flows. Ownership reframes everything: it imposes responsibilities, shapes expectations, and extends your horizon.

Yet many approach stocks as if they were commodities for instant profit—buying and selling in response to headlines, tweets, or hunches. They forget the underlying business. Price becomes the story, but price is not reality; it is only what someone is willing to pay at a given moment. True value resides deeper, requiring diligence, patience, and emotional composure.

Herein lies the central paradox of investing: technical tools are abundant, yet behavioural tools are often neglected. Most failures arise not from lack of information, but from emotional missteps—panic in downturns, greed in rallies, hesitation at opportunity. Markets move not only on earnings or macroeconomic indicators, but on moods: confidence, anxiety, momentum, and story. In this sense, the market is less a spreadsheet than a crowd.

This is not a flaw; it is the system's defining feature. The market externalises psychology, revealing not just corporate health, but investor temperament. Fear depresses prices, optimism inflates them. Movements are neither inherently good nor bad—they are human. Understanding this offers an edge: not by predicting the next swing, but by detaching from the compulsion to act. Observation, preparation, and measured positioning replace reactive behaviour.

Self-awareness is thus your most critical tool. Before purchasing your first share, understand yourself. What is your tolerance for uncertainty? How do you respond to losses? Are your decisions driven more by fear of missing out or fear of losing? Do you over-research in search of false certainty, or under-research, relying on instinct? These are practical questions; their answers shape strategy, resilience, and outcomes.

To aid this, later sections provide journaling prompts and reflection exercises—not indulgences, but instruments to build an "internal investing compass," a framework of principles that anchors you amid noise and volatility. This compass allows you to invest with intention: you begin to write your own narratives rather than outsource thinking to pundits, algorithms, or forums. You ask discerning questions: Does this business make sense to me? Does it possess a durable advantage? Could it thrive a decade hence? You build conviction, not perfection.

Conviction is clarity of reasoning, not certainty. It separates investors from speculators. Speculators chase short-term movement, follow crowds, obsess over timing. Investors seek long-term value, evidence over hype, patience over urgency.

This chapter is about that shift—from reacting to reflecting, from noise to narrative, from symbols to substance. The stock market is not something that happens to you; it is a system you participate in, shape, and learn from. It is a mirror—of economy, society, and self. The clearer your view, the more effectively you can navigate it.

Throughout, you will encounter examples that illustrate these principles—from the 17th-century Dutch tulip mania to modern meme stocks, from Warren Buffett's patient strategies to retail investors facing their first bear market. These are case studies in psychology, philosophy, and strategy, revealing how myths form, bubbles expand, and grounded thinking prevails.

We also examine how media and technology distort perception, and how financial institutions have reinforced the casino metaphor. The aim is not cynicism, but consciousness: to understand the market, not to outwit it.

Intellectual humility is key. No one predicts the future with certainty, but preparation comes from long-term thinking, resisting hype, and disciplined action. This chapter builds that foundation—not through predictions, but by establishing a mental framework that remains useful across changing conditions.

By the end, you will distinguish speculation from ownership, perceive the market as a system rather than a casino, and approach investing with intention rather than impulse. This is not merely the study of stock selection—it is the cultivation of clarity, conviction, and agency. The market becomes a mirror, reflecting not only prices, but possibilities: for growth, wisdom, and enduring influence.

Speculation, Storytelling, and the Myths We Inherit

If you want to understand someone's relationship with money, don't start with their bank statement—start with their stories. Not the stories they tell others, but the ones they've inherited, often unconsciously, about wealth, risk, success, and loss. These narratives, passed down through families, shaped by culture, and amplified by media, are not merely decorative. They are directive. They whisper in moments of decision, influence when we act and when we hesitate, and form the invisible architecture of our financial behaviour.

Investing is commonly framed as a technical skill—an exercise in valuation, analysis, and strategy. But beneath the surface lies something far more influential: psychology layered with narrative. And unless these narratives are brought into the light, no amount of tactical knowledge will override their pull. You cannot build a sound investment philosophy on top of unexamined myths.

Consider, for example, the idea that investing is a form of gambling. It's a belief many carry—sometimes implicitly, sometimes with defiance. Often it originates in families where financial security was scarce or volatile. In such environments, stability is prized, and anything involving risk is viewed with suspicion. The stock market, to those who have only seen it from the outside, becomes synonymous with recklessness. It is spoken of in hushed tones: "You could lose everything." "It's not for people like us." "Stick to what you know."

What's striking is how resilient these ideas are, even across generations. A parent who mistrusted markets because of the 2008 financial crisis may raise a child who, despite living in a more robust economy, still approaches investing with anxiety. The past casts a long shadow, especially when it comes to financial trauma. In such households, risk is not a tool—it's a threat. And when that belief hardens into identity, it becomes a kind of financial fate: I am not an investor. That's for *them.*

Contrast this with the myth of the maverick. This story, no less problematic, casts the investor as a kind of renegade genius—someone who outsmarts the crowd, picks the next unicorn, and walks away with a fortune. It is the narrative popularised by media profiles, online forums, and glossy autobiographies. It thrives on the illusion of control and exceptionalism. The danger here is not fear, but ego. Rather than avoid investing, this myth drives people to engage for the wrong reasons—to chase status, to perform intelligence, to prove something. In both cases—fear or fantasy—the result is the same: distorted decision-making.

The common thread between these opposing myths is that they crowd out reality. Investing becomes not a process of thoughtful engagement with the real economy, but a stage on which unconscious beliefs play out. You're not investing—you're acting out a story.

But stories can be rewritten. The first step is recognising them.

Cultural context plays a significant role in shaping these narratives. In the United Kingdom, for example, attitudes toward ownership and markets have long been shaped by class dynamics and property tradition. For many, the idea of owning shares is abstract compared to the tangible appeal of owning a home. Property is visible, celebrated, legitimised through law and society. Stocks, by contrast, are often seen as speculative—belonging to the world of bankers, not everyday workers.

In contrast, in the United States, a culture of financial individualism and stock market participation runs deeper. The "401(k) generation" has grown up with investing as a quasi-civic duty, embedded in retirement planning and employer schemes. Yet even here, myths abound—particularly the seductive belief that one big win can set you up for life. The lottery mindset persists, just dressed in the language of tech IPOs and cryptocurrencies.

These cultural mythologies aren't fixed. They evolve with economic events. After the dot-com bust of the early 2000s, a wave of scepticism swept through retail investors. After the 2008 crisis, many millennials delayed investing altogether. More recently, the pandemic-era bull market pulled in a new generation, fuelled by Reddit threads and meme stocks, some of whom now confront the psychological whiplash of market downturns. What connects all these moments is not just market volatility, but *narrative volatility*. When the dominant story changes, so do behaviours.

It's tempting to believe that we're immune to these forces—that if we're rational enough, informed enough, disciplined enough, we can rise above them. But that belief is itself a kind of myth. Every investor brings baggage to the table. The difference lies in whether you're aware of it.

This is where introspection becomes an investment tool—not in a metaphorical sense, but as a practical advantage. Before you analyse companies, you must analyse your own tendencies. Before you track dividends, you should track your emotional reactions. Why do you feel compelled to check your portfolio three times a day? Why does the thought of missing out on a rising stock create tension in your chest? Why do you hesitate before buying, even after research? These are not idle questions. They reveal your underlying financial scripts—and those scripts determine outcomes more often than spreadsheets do.

To begin this work, you might consider a set of journaling prompts not commonly found in investment guides: *What was money like growing up in your household? What messages did your parents or guardians communicate—explicitly or not—about wealth, risk, and ownership? How do you define financial success? Whose approval matters in your financial decisions?*

Such reflection is not therapy. It's strategy. Because once you can name the myth, you can question it. And once you can question it, you create space to choose a different way of thinking.

The transition from unconscious narrative to intentional action is where real investing begins. It shifts the question from *What should I buy?* to *What do I believe about money?* And that belief, if rooted in clarity rather than fear or fantasy, becomes the bedrock of your financial decisions.

This shift also helps explain why two people can look at the same market conditions and behave completely differently. One sees a downturn and thinks, *It's all rigged, I knew I shouldn't have done this.* Another sees the same event and thinks, *This is part of the cycle. I'm sticking to my plan.* The difference isn't intelligence—it's narrative. One is acting from inherited fear; the other from cultivated understanding.

There is also an ethical dimension to these myths, often overlooked. The stories we internalise about money are not only personal—they shape our views about others. If we believe that wealth comes only from luck or manipulation, we may resent those who have it. If we believe that anyone can get rich with enough effort, we may lack compassion for those who don't. These stories influence not only our investing behaviour but our social and political worldview. That is why examining them is not merely self-help—it is civic responsibility.

In practical terms, deconstructing these myths enables better strategy. It helps you define your risk profile more accurately, distinguish between long-term investing and short-term gambling, and build a portfolio that reflects your values rather than inherited anxieties. It allows you to commit to holding periods, to stick with companies during volatility, to avoid panic-selling, and to walk away from hype cycles. It gives you resilience—not just financial, but psychological.

Moreover, this work inoculates you against the manipulations of marketing and media. When you understand the stories you're carrying, you're less susceptible to the stories being sold. You're not swayed by every expert prediction, nor paralysed by each dip. You have a centre—a set of internal convictions stronger than external noise.

Ultimately, investing is not about escaping emotion. It's about learning which emotions to trust. And that discernment comes not from suppressing your financial stories, but from understanding them deeply. You cannot become a wise investor without becoming, in some sense, a wise interpreter of narrative—your own and others'.

Speculation thrives on unexamined myth. It feeds on fear, fantasy, and urgency. Ownership, by contrast, requires clarity. It asks for a kind of psychological posture: calm, curious, sceptical, but not cynical. When you invest from ownership, you are not just trying to beat the market. You are trying to align your capital with your convictions. That is a harder path—but also a more durable one.

You will not get there by mimicking others. You will not get there by memorising tactics. You will get there by seeing more clearly—starting with the stories that shaped you, and choosing, step by step, to write a better one.

What a Share Really Is: More Than a Price Tag

When most people hear the word "stock," what they imagine is closer to a number than a thing. A line on a screen. A price that moves. A symbol—often three or four letters—that flashes red or green, inviting either panic or greed. The cultural shorthand for investing has become so compressed that a share is rarely seen as what it truly is. It is reduced to price movement, stripped of context, and reimagined as a kind of tradeable unit of speculation. But a share is not a bet. It is not a number detached from substance. It is not even primarily a financial instrument. A share, in its essence, is *ownership*. And not ownership in the abstract—but in a real, breathing, evolving enterprise.

This distinction matters. Because how you *see* a share determines how you treat it. If it is just a price, you will chase it when it rises and abandon it when it falls. If it is just a trade, you will measure its value in seconds, not years. But if it is a stake in a business—if it represents your part-ownership in the machinery of production, service, innovation, or global distribution—then your decisions take on different dimensions. You begin to think like an owner, not a speculator. And that shift is foundational to long-term wealth creation.

To grasp what a share really is, consider what happens when a company first offers its stock to the public. An initial public offering (IPO) is not a magic trick—it is a sale of ownership. The founders, early investors, and executives decide to make a portion of the business available to outside participants. In doing so, they invite the public to share in the company's future success—or failure. When you buy one of those shares, you are not purchasing a promise of profit. You are acquiring a small slice of the entire enterprise: its assets, liabilities, brand, customer base, intellectual property, workforce, and leadership.

This is not mere semantics. It's the legal and economic foundation of the stock market. When you own shares, you are a shareholder—entitled, at scale, to voting rights, dividend distributions, and a claim on future earnings. You are not renting potential upside. You are purchasing a proportional seat at the table, even if your influence is small. The value of that seat is not determined solely by market perception, but by the underlying strength and direction of the business itself.

Take Apple as an example. When you buy a share in Apple, you are buying into a company with factories, patents, employees, relationships with suppliers, marketing strategies, and customer loyalty built over decades. That single share reflects the present and projected value of all those components. Its price may fluctuate daily, but its worth—the stream of cash flows it can generate over time—is rooted in the company's operations. To ignore this is to confuse *price* with *value*, which is the foundational error of many novice investors.

It's important to underline how dangerous that confusion can be. Price is immediate, reactive, and emotional. It moves with news cycles, investor sentiment, and market momentum. Value, by contrast, is cumulative, patient, and often invisible in the short term. If your entire engagement with the stock market is framed through prices, you will forever be reacting to surface-level turbulence. But if you root your attention in value, you begin to develop an investment philosophy based on discernment rather than distraction.

This requires a mindset shift from viewing stocks as lottery tickets to treating them as long-term business partnerships. Warren Buffett, arguably the most disciplined investor of our time, has long advocated this perspective. He famously remarked that if you wouldn't be happy owning a stock for ten years, you shouldn't consider holding it for ten minutes. This isn't an endorsement of inertia—it's a statement about perspective. When you buy a share, you are entering into an agreement: I believe in this company's capacity to grow, adapt, and deliver value over time. That belief should be grounded in understanding—not rumour, hype, or hope.

Of course, understanding a business takes effort. But that effort is precisely what separates intentional investing from speculative behaviour. It means reading annual reports, understanding how the company makes money, studying its competitive position, analysing its leadership, and asking whether its future prospects justify its current price. This is not reserved for professionals. Any intelligent investor can do it—provided they see a share not as a ticker, but as a living extension of a real-world enterprise.

The reason this distinction has eroded is partly historical. With the rise of online brokerages, algorithmic trading, and financial media, the stock market has been recast in the public eye as a digital arcade—a place of constant movement, dopamine hits, and simplified interfaces. Platforms like Robinhood, with their game-like design, have further amplified this effect. By abstracting away the underlying business and focusing purely on price action, they reinforce the illusion that investing is merely about catching the next swing. The result is a generation of investors who may hold dozens of stocks but understand none of the companies they supposedly own.

This is not just a philosophical concern—it's a practical vulnerability. Investors who don't understand what they own are more likely to panic during downturns, more prone to follow the herd, and more susceptible to financial propaganda disguised as insight. They react to fear, not fundamentals. But investors who approach each stock as a stake in a real company are better positioned to ride through volatility, make rational decisions, and compound their returns over time.

There's also a behavioural dimension to this. When you think like a business owner, your time horizon expands. You become less focused on quarterly earnings and more focused on five-year strategy. You learn to evaluate a dip not as a threat but as a potential buying opportunity—provided the business itself remains healthy. You stop asking "Is this stock going up?" and start asking "Is this business worth more than I'm paying for it?" That single question reframes everything.

It also reinforces the idea that ownership involves responsibility. Even as a small shareholder, your capital is not passive. It supports the business's capacity to operate, innovate, and grow. And while you may not directly influence company policy, your decision to invest is a form of endorsement. This raises important ethical considerations. What do the businesses you own stand for? How do they treat their workers, their communities, and the environment? Are their profits derived from practices you believe in? These are not abstract concerns for large institutional investors alone. They belong to anyone who sees investing as a practice of alignment, not just accumulation.

This deeper engagement also inoculates you against the temptations of constant trading. The financial industry thrives on activity—every transaction generates fees, even if minimal. But ownership is about continuity, not churn. The best returns in history have often come from buying high-quality companies and holding them for long periods, through cycles of boom and bust. That only works if you *believe* in what you own—and belief is hard to sustain without understanding.

There is, of course, a legitimate space for short-term trading, speculation, and arbitrage. But those are specialised activities, often requiring a level of speed, data access, and emotional detachment that most individual investors cannot and should not try to replicate. The noise of price movements can seduce even the most rational mind. But the clarity of business fundamentals remains the enduring compass.

As you refine your investing approach, consider adopting a filter: before buying a share, ask yourself whether you would still want to own the underlying business if you could never sell the stock for five years. Would you be comfortable with that level of commitment? Does the company's business model make sense to you? Can you explain how it makes money in a few sentences? Do you understand its risks, its competitors, and its growth drivers? These questions slow you down—not to paralyse decision-making, but to ensure it's built on solid ground.

Thinking in terms of ownership also helps clarify your portfolio construction. You stop viewing diversification as merely buying different stocks. Instead, you see it as owning a range of distinct businesses across industries, geographies, and revenue models. Each one has its own risk profile, cash flow dynamics, and strategic outlook. This mental model encourages a healthier relationship with investing—one rooted in realism, discernment, and proportionality.

By reimagining a share as what it truly is—partial ownership in a living, evolving business—you anchor your financial decisions in the world of real consequences. You move beyond ticker symbols and into the world of factories, software teams, logistics chains, customer retention strategies, and competitive moats. You begin to see the economy not as a blur of numbers, but as a vast, interconnected network of enterprises—some enduring, some fading, all competing for relevance and reward.

This view won't guarantee returns. But it will ground your approach. It will give you a framework that holds under stress, a sense of direction amid volatility, and a deeper connection to what your money is actually doing. That is not a small thing. It is the foundation of wise investing—and it begins with seeing past the price.

Markets as Collective Psychology

The greatest illusion in investing is that the market is purely rational. We imagine it as a neutral mechanism: a machine that aggregates data, processes information, and spits out fair prices. But beneath the numbers, beneath the indices and earnings reports, lies something far messier—emotion, perception, and human bias operating at scale. The stock market is not an algorithm detached from humanity. It is a *crowd*, and crowds are not rational entities. They are reactive, volatile, and profoundly psychological. To understand the market is to understand how human beings behave in groups—how we think, fear, hope, and herd.

This is not a poetic framing. It is a functional truth. Prices, after all, are set at the margin—where one person is willing to buy and another is willing to sell. Those decisions are not made in a vacuum. They are made in response to news, narratives, incentives, and internal states—excitement, anxiety, overconfidence, doubt. The result is that markets often move not on fundamentals, but on *feelings about fundamentals*. And when enough people feel strongly in the same direction, those feelings become self-reinforcing.

Consider the dot-com bubble of the late 1990s. Companies with no revenue and unproven business models saw their valuations soar simply because they had ".com" in their name. Investors, fuelled by FOMO and techno-optimism, justified astronomical valuations with vague appeals to the future. It was not that they believed profits didn't matter—they believed profits would come later, that growth was destiny, and that scepticism meant missing out. That belief wasn't isolated. It became communal. The market, collectively, told itself a story—and behaved accordingly. When the narrative cracked, the sell-off was brutal. The same psychology flipped. Fear replaced greed. People rushed to exit not because companies changed overnight, but because the mood changed. The market became a mirror of emotional contagion.

This is not an exception. It is a pattern. We saw it again in the housing bubble of the mid-2000s, and again—more recently—with meme stocks like GameStop and AMC. In each case, prices became detached from underlying business realities, driven instead by sentiment, social dynamics, and narrative momentum. The tools were different—Reddit threads instead of brokerage newsletters—but the emotional mechanics were the same. A critical mass of belief leads to collective movement, which reinforces belief, until the weight of reality intervenes.

Understanding this gives you a profound advantage—not by allowing you to predict the next wave, but by helping you *detach* from it. Most investors are not undone by ignorance. They are undone by overreaction. When you see the market through the lens of collective psychology, you stop expecting it to behave sensibly at all times. You stop expecting perfect alignment between price and value, and you stop taking short-term movements personally. That detachment is not cynicism. It is composure.

This does not mean that fundamentals don't matter. They matter deeply—over the long term. But between now and then, the market may swing wildly based on non-fundamental forces: interest rate whispers, inflation forecasts, political drama, and viral narratives. These movements often defy logic, but not psychology. Because while each investor may think they are acting independently, they are often responding to the same stimuli—headlines, price charts, peer pressure, and social cues. This is where behavioural finance, still too often treated as a side dish, becomes essential.

The foundational insight of behavioural finance is that humans are not always rational actors. We are loss-averse, prone to confirmation bias, anchored by past prices, and overconfident in our forecasting abilities. When you scale these traits across millions of market participants, you get volatility that reflects *human nature* more than economic reality. This is why markets overreact to bad news and then overcorrect. It's why people buy high and sell low, despite knowing they shouldn't. It's why fear spreads faster than fact, and why bubbles always seem obvious—*after* they've burst.

George Soros, one of the most successful traders of the 20th century, built his investment philosophy around this premise. His concept of *reflexivity* challenged the traditional view that markets tend toward equilibrium. Instead, he argued, markets are influenced by the perceptions of participants, which in turn shape outcomes. If enough people believe a stock will rise, they buy it, which causes it to rise—validating the belief, at least temporarily. This feedback loop doesn't necessarily reflect reality. It reflects consensus belief, which may or may not align with the truth.

The key, then, is not to exit the market because it is emotional, but to *navigate it* with emotional awareness. Most investors attempt to solve uncertainty with prediction. They pore over forecasts, trying to anticipate the next move. But this approach often backfires. The more you try to predict short-term movements, the more entangled you become in the same psychological traps that drive irrational behaviour. A better strategy is to accept uncertainty as a feature, not a flaw. Rather than trying to *control* the market, learn to *understand* its moods—and to separate those moods from your own.

This requires developing a psychological immune system. It means being able to watch your portfolio decline in value without panic. It means resisting the urge to buy simply because others are buying. It means avoiding the trap of thinking that everyone else knows something you don't. The irony is that the crowd often acts not on superior information, but on amplified emotion. Emotional detachment, in this context, is not indifference. It is a cultivated discipline.

Cultivating that discipline involves building routines and rules that distance you from reactive decision-making. This might include checking your portfolio on a set schedule rather than daily, keeping an investment journal to track your thinking, or defining clear criteria for buying and selling in advance. These practices aren't just helpful—they're necessary. Because once you're in the middle of a panic or frenzy, it's too late to build clarity. You have to build it *before* the wave hits.

It also means having a clear philosophy—an internal compass that's stronger than the market's mood. Are you investing for income, growth, stability, or a blend? What kind of businesses do you want to own? What is your time horizon? What are your personal thresholds for risk? These questions aren't abstract. They are anchors. They prevent you from being swept into the collective emotional tides that move the market.

And yet, even with all this, detachment does not mean disengagement. One of the more subtle dangers in understanding market psychology is the temptation toward superiority. Once you see how irrational markets can be, it's easy to feel above it all—to sneer at the crowd and assume your detachment makes you immune. But that, too, is a trap. It replaces fear with arrogance, and both are dangerous. The goal is not to remove yourself from the market's emotional ecosystem, but to participate with humility and awareness.

There is also an ethical dimension to this awareness. If markets are driven by emotion as much as data, then narratives matter. Stories about innovation, crisis, or transformation shape capital flows—and those flows have real-world consequences. They influence which businesses thrive, which industries attract funding, and which ideas get scaled. As investors, we are not merely observers of market psychology—we are contributors to it. Every decision reinforces or challenges the collective narrative. Understanding this can help you become a more intentional investor—less reactive, more reflective, and ultimately more responsible.

You don't have to be a behavioural economist to benefit from this insight. You just have to recognise that the market is not a spreadsheet—it's a crowd. And crowds behave differently from individuals. They amplify certain voices, ignore inconvenient truths, and swing between extremes. But within that noise lies opportunity—not necessarily for timing the market, but for staying rational when others aren't.

This is what Warren Buffett meant when he said, "Be fearful when others are greedy, and greedy when others are fearful." It's not a slogan. It's a behavioural principle. It recognises that markets often overshoot in both directions. If you can resist the pull of the crowd at its extremes, you give yourself the space to act with reason.

That space is where long-term wealth is built—not in perfectly predicting movements, but in consistently making sound decisions while others are being pulled by psychological currents they don't fully understand. Your edge is not superior forecasting. It's superior temperament.

And that temperament begins with a new kind of seeing—noticing when markets are no longer trading on facts but on feelings, recognising when sentiment is divorced from substance, and choosing not to follow simply because the crowd is moving.

Markets are not machines. They are mirrors—reflecting back our collective hopes, fears, delusions, and insights. When you stop expecting the mirror to always reflect reality, you free yourself to see it more clearly. And when you see clearly, you act wisely. That is how psychology becomes not a weakness, but an advantage.

The Inner Game of Investing Begins Before the First Trade

The hardest part of investing isn't choosing what to buy—it's managing *yourself*. Long before your money enters the market, your mind already has. Your beliefs, your fears, your self-concept, your need for certainty or control—these are the forces shaping every financial decision, whether or not you're conscious of them. The charts, ratios, and forecasts come later. The real game begins with your psychology. And unless you're prepared to understand and regulate it, no amount of knowledge will compensate for the behaviour it undermines.

The world doesn't lack for information. You can, within minutes, access price histories, analyst reports, insider trades, and financial models. Yet most investors, even with all this at their fingertips, still underperform. The reason isn't data—it's discipline. And discipline is a function of mindset. More specifically, it's a function of knowing how your own thinking operates under pressure, uncertainty, and temptation. *Investing is 80% mental composition, and only 20% technical competence.* That ratio may seem inflated to the technically minded, but the evidence suggests otherwise.

Behavioural finance, now a well-established field thanks to scholars like Daniel Kahneman, Amos Tversky, and Richard Thaler, has repeatedly shown that the gap between what people *know* and what they *do* is wide. Investors regularly buy high and sell low, ignore their own risk tolerance, overtrade, or freeze in moments when action would help. These mistakes are not failures of intellect. They are the predictable outcomes of unmanaged emotion, unchecked bias, and unexamined narratives. Knowing how to avoid these pitfalls requires more than memorising behavioural terms—it demands honest introspection.

This is why the process of becoming an investor must start before your first trade. Not with research on companies, but with research on yourself. What kind of investor are you trying to become? What kind of risks can you genuinely stomach? How do you respond to volatility, ambiguity, and loss? What does wealth mean to you—not in theory, but in practice? These are not soft questions. They are the scaffolding upon which all of your future investing decisions will rest. Get them wrong, and your strategy will fracture the moment the market turns against you.

Journaling—systematic, intentional, non-performative writing—can play a crucial role in uncovering your internal architecture. It allows you to surface subconscious patterns, test assumptions, and confront contradictions. But not all journaling is equally useful. You need prompts that cut through generalities and elicit specifics. Prompts that challenge easy answers and create enough discomfort to be revealing. For example:

What is your earliest memory involving money? What emotions are attached to it?

How did your family talk—or not talk—about investing? What messages did you absorb from that silence or speech?

When have you felt the most regret about a financial decision? What triggered the decision at the time?

How do you define financial safety? Is it a number, a feeling, or a relationship to control?

If the market dropped 30% tomorrow, what would you do—and how do you know?

Would you rather miss out on a major gain or suffer a major loss? Why?

These prompts are not academic exercises. They are diagnostic tools. Your answers may change over time, but the point is to start building a map of your emotional terrain. Without that map, you're navigating blind—and the market is a dangerous place to fly on instinct.

There's also value in identifying your specific cognitive biases in advance. Everyone has them, but their expression is personal. Some investors are prone to *overconfidence bias*, believing they can time the market or spot trends before others. Others fall prey to *loss aversion*, overreacting to small losses and abandoning long-term plans at the first sign of downturn. Still others struggle with *confirmation bias*, cherry-picking information that supports their thesis while ignoring contrary evidence. Knowing which traps you're likely to fall into allows you to build mechanisms—checklists, second opinions, cooling-off periods—to reduce their influence.

Risk tolerance, often misunderstood as a static trait, is also highly context-dependent. It's not just a question of "How much can you afford to lose?" but "How much uncertainty can you emotionally tolerate while still making rational decisions?" Theoretical risk tolerance tends to be inflated when markets are calm and abstract. The real test comes during turbulence. That's when investors discover whether they were building castles on confidence or bedrock.

This is why simulations and mental rehearsals are useful. Before investing, ask yourself what you would do if your portfolio fell 20%. Not what you *should* do, but what you *would* do, based on past behaviour and emotional patterning. If the answer is "I'd probably panic and sell," then it's wise to adjust your asset allocation now—before that moment arrives. Building an investing identity isn't about bracing for worst-case scenarios with bravado. It's about designing your strategy to accommodate your actual temperament—not your ideal self-image.

That self-image deserves closer scrutiny. Many new investors construct identities around competence, trying to emulate the habits of admired figures—Buffett, Bogle, Dalio—as if mimicry alone will yield results. But what's often missing is an honest confrontation with one's own motivations. Are you investing to grow wealth, or to prove something? Are you hoping to be admired for your insight, or to cultivate long-term independence? Do you see investing as a discipline to master—or as a lever to escape something else?

This reflective work is difficult, not because it's intellectually complex, but because it requires emotional honesty. It involves confronting your financial fears, naming your blind spots, and stepping outside the performance of competence that so often clouds judgment. But it's this process—not a stock screen, not a technical chart—that gives you an edge in the real world. Because while information is abundant, *perspective* is scarce. And perspective is what allows you to hold your ground when others are losing theirs.

This isn't a one-time exercise. Your mindset will evolve as your life circumstances change—career shifts, family responsibilities, health events, or broader economic developments will all alter your perception of risk, time, and reward. The challenge is not to fix your mindset permanently, but to *stay in active dialogue with it.* Regular journaling, periodic reassessment of your values, and reviewing past decisions with an eye for pattern—not blame—create a feedback loop that keeps your investing aligned with your evolving self.

There's also the matter of *time preference*—how you value immediate rewards versus future gains. This is not merely theoretical. It's the psychological foundation of delayed gratification, and by extension, of compounding returns. If you struggle to resist short-term impulses, you will find it hard to benefit from long-term investing—even if you intellectually believe in it. Building the capacity for delayed reward is not a moral achievement. It's a strategic advantage. And like any skill, it can be trained—through rituals, constraints, and intentional design of your investing environment.

That design matters more than most realise. Behaviour is often shaped less by intention than by environment. If your phone notifies you every time a stock moves, your emotional state is constantly primed for reactivity. If your investing app feels like a game, you'll treat it like one. But if you create friction—if trades require deliberation, if you track your rationale before acting, if you have trusted frameworks in place—you give your rational mind a fighting chance against the rush of impulsivity.

What this all adds up to is simple, though rarely stated directly: *you are the main risk to your portfolio.* Not the market, not inflation, not geopolitical instability. Those are all variables to consider, but the most consistent threat to long-term success is the undisciplined investor—the one who panics, overtrades, chases fads, or fails to adapt. The one who reacts instead of reflects. And the antidote to that risk is *not more information.* It is *better self-knowledge.*

That knowledge isn't glamorous. It doesn't lend itself to charts or flashy predictions. But it builds resilience. It allows you to operate with composure when others are spiralling. It helps you stick to your plan when conditions change. It ensures that your portfolio isn't just a random collection of assets, but a coherent expression of your values, your priorities, and your lived understanding of risk.

If investing is a discipline—as this book insists it is—then it must begin with the internal. Before the first trade, before the first research report, before the first dividend hits your account, there is mindset. That is the raw material from which your financial future is shaped. Refine it, and you build not only wealth, but wisdom. And wisdom, unlike wealth, cannot be taken from you.

Chapter 2
Choosing Your First Act of Ownership

At some point, the abstract concept of investing collides with reality. You've reflected on your beliefs, interrogated inherited financial myths, and begun to grasp the psychological currents that shape markets—and now the moment arrives to act. Theory must meet practice. In this quiet, decisive threshold, a subtle but profound shift occurs: you cease to be a mere observer of the financial world. You are preparing to step into it—not by chasing headlines or gambling on whims, but by establishing the infrastructure through which your long-term philosophy can function. This chapter focuses on that first tangible act of ownership: opening a brokerage account.

It may seem mundane, even bureaucratic, but it is profoundly philosophical. Not because the paperwork or verification is complex—it is not—but because the choice of how you enter the market reflects your relationship with autonomy, your tolerance for complexity, and your capacity to act with deliberation amid noise. In an era where platforms compete for attention, offering frictionless access and seductive interfaces, choosing a brokerage becomes a test of intentionality. The objective is not merely to begin; it is to begin well, with clarity and alignment.

This chapter is not a catalogue of platforms or a tutorial on software navigation. Those resources are abundant and quickly obsolete. What matters is the underlying frame: what are you really selecting when you choose a brokerage? What trade-offs are implicit in your choice? Which aspects will you automate, and which will remain reserved for human judgment? These are the questions that define the kind of investor this book is guiding you to become.

Structurally, direct investment in stocks is not possible. You cannot walk into a market and purchase shares like groceries. A brokerage functions as the portal between your capital and the global market. But this portal is far from neutral. Each carries design biases, incentives, and user-interface cues: some favour passive investing, others encourage high-frequency trading. Some platforms offer minimalist designs that respect focus; others gamify interactions, layering noise atop novelty. The choice of platform is thus inseparable from the environment in which your investment practice will operate.

Environment shapes behaviour. A brokerage that floods you with alerts, promotes "top movers," or showers confetti for every trade is not merely providing access—it is conditioning you to act as a trader, not an owner. The right platform reinforces the type of investor you aspire to be rather than undermining focus.

Psychological depth enters here. If simplicity and automation matter to you, prioritise recurring deposits, fractional shares, and long-term portfolio tools. If granular control is your preference, seek robust research capabilities and transparent execution. Yet even these surface preferences should be weighed against your deeper motives. Do you crave control out of anxiety, or from deliberate reflection on sustainable engagement?

Consider the practicalities across different jurisdictions. In the United States, Fidelity or Charles Schwab require a Social Security Number, identity proof, and bank linkage. Robinhood, popular among younger investors, has design elements that encourage frequent trading. In Canada, Wealthsimple and Questrade offer TFSA and RRSP accounts, each with distinct tax implications. German investors typically use PostIdent verification for platforms like Trade Republic or Scalable Capital. In India, electronic KYC linked to Aadhaar and PAN is needed, alongside Demat and Trading accounts via Zerodha or Groww. Japan presents language and verification barriers, making local brokers such as SBI or Rakuten preferable.

The lesson is not to memorise these processes, but to recognise a broader truth: investing is embedded within systems. Each jurisdiction reflects regulatory values, cultural attitudes to risk, and implicit definitions of what investing should achieve. Navigating this landscape requires maintaining psychological grounding. You are not merely entering a system; you are establishing a personal financial practice that demands patience, ritual, and self-awareness.

Even after opening an account, new investors often experience paralysis. Choice overwhelms: which account type, which stocks, how often to check, what if a decision goes wrong? This is the paradox of choice—excess options breed anxiety. Response is often either hasty action or paralysis.

One solution is pre-designing a high-quality decision environment. Constraints can liberate rather than restrict. Limit speculative investments to a set proportion of your portfolio. Commit to quarterly reviews rather than daily monitoring. Build a shortlist of companies you understand, and restrict selections to that pool until your knowledge deepens. Confidence grows not through exposure to infinite options, but through repetition of thoughtful choices.

Automation, too, is an ally—not as a substitute for judgment, but as a tool to reduce friction and prevent impulsive behaviour. Regular contributions remove the temptation to time markets. Yet automation must be intentional: funding can be automated, but selection, evaluation, and exit decisions remain human. A half-mechanical, half-conscious system delivers both consistency and responsiveness.

Finally, this chapter emphasises the creation of a Personal Investment Manifesto. This is no vision board or performance checklist. It is a written statement of values, principles, and enduring priorities to consult when markets turn chaotic or enticing. It might articulate ideas such as: "I invest to create freedom, not status." "I do not panic-sell unless fundamentals change." "I ignore media predictions." Or practical allocations: "70% global index funds, 20% dividend-paying companies I understand, 10% emerging technologies for research."

Why write it down? Because memory fails under stress. Your future self, confronted by volatility, needs guidance from the present self, grounded in reason and clarity. A manifesto acts as a lighthouse in fog, preventing drift.

Opening a brokerage account is thus far more than a procedural step—it is a foundational act of identity. The choices you make in platform, automation, limits, and values shape the trajectory of your investing practice. Perfection on day one is not the aim; fidelity to clarity is.

Mechanics will follow. You will buy your first share, then another. Markets will fluctuate. But the character of your investing has been established—not through trades, but through beliefs. This chapter is about initiating that character: opening not just an account, but a long-term relationship with intentional ownership.

Opening a Brokerage Account Without Losing Yourself

The technical act of opening a brokerage account is simple—verifying your identity, linking a bank, selecting an account type. But wrapped within that simplicity is a subtle yet critical moment of identity formation. This is not just paperwork. It is the beginning of your engagement with the architecture of financial ownership. And like most beginnings, it can either be conscious and empowering—or reactive, vague, and shaped by forces you don't fully understand. The challenge isn't merely functional. It's psychological. How do you move from interest to action without surrendering your focus to convenience, marketing, or decision fatigue?

What makes this process uniquely demanding is not the difficulty of the forms, but the illusion that this first step is purely administrative. It's not. The platform you choose, the features you prioritise, the friction you accept or eliminate—these will shape your behaviour long after you've forgotten why you chose them in the first place. Platforms are not passive intermediaries. They are behavioural environments. And environments shape outcomes.

Let's begin with the obvious: you need a brokerage account to buy shares. But *how* you go about opening that account depends on where you live, what your objectives are, and—most importantly—what kind of investor you want to become. Every country has its own regulatory ecosystem, ID requirements, account types, and tax implications. But across geographies, one principle remains constant: your brokerage is not just a service provider. It is your *financial practice partner.* You're not merely opening an account. You're defining the space in which your investment behaviour will unfold.

In the United States, the dominant players—Fidelity, Charles Schwab, and Robinhood—each offer low-fee trading and a frictionless onboarding process. A Social Security Number, proof of identity, and a linked bank account are enough to get started. But here the divergence begins. Fidelity and Schwab are built with long-term investors in mind. Their interfaces are clean, their educational resources extensive, and their culture oriented toward stability. Robinhood, by contrast, despite its zero-commission model, has come under criticism for its gamified interface. Confetti graphics, swipe-to-trade functionality, and lists of "hot stocks" encourage frequency rather than deliberation. If your temperament is drawn toward action, Robinhood may not be your ally—it may be your enabler. This is not a question of right or wrong, but of psychological fit. *You must choose a platform that protects you from your worst tendencies, not one that exploits them.*

In Canada, Questrade and Wealthsimple offer intuitive digital onboarding via SIN verification, identity documents, and a linked bank account. The core decision for Canadians isn't just which platform to use, but which account type to prioritise: a Tax-Free Savings Account (TFSA) or a Registered Retirement Savings Plan (RRSP). Each has tax implications. A TFSA allows for tax-free growth and withdrawals, making it ideal for flexible, medium-term investing. An RRSP, by contrast, provides upfront tax deductions but taxes withdrawals later, aligning more with long-term retirement planning. The right choice depends on your income profile, time horizon, and liquidity needs. The wrong choice isn't disastrous—but it is often irreversible in the short term. *This is where financial intention begins—not with trades, but with structure.*

In Germany, opening an account with Trade Republic or Scalable Capital requires a Tax ID, IBAN, and identity verification through PostIdent or similar services. These platforms are highly streamlined, with mobile-first interfaces and low-cost structures. What sets the German market apart is the prevalence of savings plans (*Sparpläne*), where users automate monthly investments into ETFs or stocks. This can be an enormous behavioural asset, especially for first-time investors. It converts investment into routine, not reaction. But automation is only useful when it aligns with understanding. If you don't know what you own—or why—it's not a strategy, it's a default setting.

In India, platforms like Zerodha and Groww have radically simplified retail investing through e-KYC processes linked to Aadhaar and PAN. The two-account structure—Demat and Trading—can seem confusing at first, but serves a clear purpose: Demat holds your securities, Trading facilitates their purchase. Once verification is complete, users can fund accounts via UPI or net banking and begin trading. But the ease of access hides a deeper complexity: most new investors are not prepared for the overwhelming volume of options available on these platforms. The temptation to trade frequently is ever-present. The responsibility, therefore, is not just regulatory—it is *cognitive.* You must bring a plan to the platform, or the platform will give you one by default. That plan will likely be driven by novelty and noise.

Japan presents its own nuances. Brokerages like SBI and Rakuten require a My Number identity submission, proof of residency, and a local bank account. Japanese platforms are often less anglicised, with interfaces and support predominantly in Japanese. This linguistic and procedural barrier can be frustrating for newcomers—but it also slows the process, forcing greater deliberation. And slowness, in investing, is underrated. It builds pause. It encourages alignment. *The delay between desire and execution can be protective.*

Across all regions, the selection of a brokerage is not just about functionality—it's about *fit.* Some platforms are designed for speed, others for stability. Some are sleek, others are comprehensive. The right platform for you is not the one that impresses others, but the one that supports *your specific behavioural architecture.* If you are prone to tinkering, choose a brokerage that requires a few more steps to place a trade. If you are likely to procrastinate, select one that automates deposits and makes portfolio tracking intuitive. This is not about hacking your willpower. It is about designing your financial environment to *reinforce your intentions.*

This is where many first-time investors go astray. They confuse accessibility with alignment. They believe that because opening an account is easy, investing must be simple. But *ease is not clarity.* A platform can give you the illusion of competence while quietly exploiting your behavioural vulnerabilities. This is not a conspiracy—it's a business model. The more you trade, the more data you generate, and the more time you spend on the platform, the more value you provide. You are the product. Recognising this doesn't mean withdrawing. It means reasserting agency.

There is another, more personal dimension to this decision. Many investors begin with the quiet hope that by opening an account, they will become someone else: someone more disciplined, more forward-looking, more financially fluent. But the account doesn't change who you are. It reveals who you already are. Your patterns—avoidance, impulsiveness, curiosity, reflection—will all show up in how you engage with your brokerage. Rather than fighting this, *observe it.* Use the early weeks not to trade incessantly, but to study yourself. What do you reach for? What do you avoid? What triggers excitement or paralysis? Your answers are the foundation of your investing identity.

To protect that identity, some friction is healthy. You don't need the fastest app or the lowest fees. You need an interface that reflects the kind of decisions you want to make. You need to create space—psychological and logistical—between impulse and action. One way to do this is to write a short pre-investment reflection for any trade above a certain amount: Why am I buying this? What do I understand about the business? What would make me sell? This isn't busywork. It's *cognitive clarity in written form*. And clarity compounds.

None of this should deter you from acting. The risk isn't that you'll make the wrong choice. The risk is that you'll make it reflexively. Your brokerage account is not just a portal. It is a container for your attention, your habits, and your evolving understanding of ownership. It is the interface through which your ideas about value, time, and responsibility will be tested. You are not just choosing a platform. You are choosing the conditions under which your financial behaviour will unfold.

Begin carefully. Begin consciously. But do begin. Because the act of opening an account, when done with intentionality, is not a minor administrative task. It is your first declaration of ownership. Not just of assets, but of *agency*. And that is where investing truly starts.

Decision Fatigue and the Paradox of Choice

The modern investor is drowning in options. Every day, countless platforms, pundits, and product providers offer a menu of possibilities—stock picks, ETFs, dividend aristocrats, thematic portfolios, robo-advisors, real-time signals, ESG filters, fractional shares, leveraged products, tax-loss harvesting tools. The sheer volume of choice, once marketed as a sign of empowerment, has quietly become an obstacle. What was meant to enable intelligent investing now threatens to erode it, not because choice is bad, but because *unbounded choice is paralysing*. Decision fatigue, a concept once confined to cognitive psychology, has found fertile ground in the financial domain—and it's undermining the very clarity that long-term investing requires.

The paradox of choice is not a metaphor. It is a measurable cognitive phenomenon. The more options we are given, the more mental effort it takes to weigh them. Eventually, the quality of our decisions deteriorates—not necessarily because we lack the knowledge to choose wisely, but because our capacity to evaluate rationally diminishes under cumulative strain. What begins as curiosity ends in depletion. This is decision fatigue, and in the context of investing, its consequences are serious: procrastination, impulsive trades, chronic second-guessing, and worse—abandonment of the process altogether.

Consider this: you sit down, motivated to begin investing. Within minutes, you're faced with 4,000 listed equities on the NYSE and NASDAQ alone. Add in global markets, ETFs, mutual funds, real estate investment trusts, and alternative assets, and your menu now runs into the tens of thousands. You've read that diversification is key, but no one has told you how to balance conviction with coverage. You try researching one sector, but quickly find conflicting opinions. You bookmark five articles, start two podcasts, and find yourself comparing Vanguard's S&P 500 ETF to BlackRock's equivalent for thirty minutes—only to abandon both and do nothing. This is not a lack of will. It is *cognitive overload.* And it is more common than most investors are willing to admit.

Ironically, the very tools designed to help investors—screeners, model portfolios, AI-driven recommendations—often exacerbate the problem. They multiply choices without improving context. They give you more options, faster, with less friction. But friction, in the right places, is not the enemy of good decision-making. It is often the ally. A well-designed investing process does not maximise access. It reduces *unnecessary mental load*, carving out space for discernment.

Part of the problem stems from a cultural misunderstanding. In many spheres of modern life, more choice is equated with more freedom. But in the domain of high-stakes decision-making—medicine, law, aviation, finance—*freedom without structure becomes a liability*. Research conducted by psychologists Sheena Iyengar and Mark Lepper famously demonstrated that people offered fewer choices not only made decisions more efficiently but also reported higher satisfaction with those decisions afterwards. Apply this to investing, and the implications are clear: clarity improves when options are *curated*, not expanded without limit.

This doesn't mean reducing your exposure to opportunity. It means structuring your environment so that each decision you face is meaningful, not noise. Start by defining a clear framework that limits your investable universe. You might decide to focus on only one asset class for your first year—say, equities—or to build a simple core-satellite structure: a globally diversified ETF as your foundation, complemented by a small, intentional basket of individual stocks you're willing to research in depth. You might commit to evaluating no more than three new companies per quarter. These aren't arbitrary constraints. They're *protective design choices*—rules that insulate you from the paralysis of perpetual consideration.

In the long term, what distinguishes successful investors is not their ability to choose the "best" stocks out of thousands. It's their ability to create and operate within a high-quality *decision environment.* This environment is marked by a few key features: a finite, self-defined list of viable options; a recurring rhythm for evaluation (e.g. quarterly portfolio reviews, not daily check-ins); written principles for buying and selling; and the psychological discipline to let most noise pass unnoticed. These conditions don't reduce your agency—they enhance it. By narrowing your scope, you deepen your analysis. By filtering out the irrelevant, you gain energy for what matters.

Contrast this with the default approach. Many new investors operate in reactive mode. They're constantly consuming information—Twitter threads, Reddit forums, CNBC tickers, Substack newsletters—believing that more input will eventually yield clarity. But the input rarely resolves itself into insight. Instead, it becomes a permanent background hum of contradiction. Every strong buy has a compelling bear case. Every sell signal is countered by a contrarian thesis. The result is a mind that never settles—exhausted, uncertain, unable to act with conviction. What's missing isn't intelligence. It's intentional architecture.

Part of designing that architecture is recognising your *decision bandwidth*—the number of quality decisions you can make in a given time before fatigue sets in. For most people, that number is lower than they'd like to admit. Behavioural economists have shown that willpower, like physical energy, is finite. After making several complex choices, our brains begin to conserve energy by defaulting to heuristics. We pick the familiar over the best. We avoid nuance. We chase certainty. This is when we start treating investing like entertainment or escape—not a practice of ownership, but a distraction from deeper discomfort.

To prevent this drift, experienced investors build systems. They standardise low-stakes decisions so that their mental bandwidth is preserved for the high-impact ones. Warren Buffett doesn't waste time on small decisions because his process filters them out. He's famously said that the key to investing is having a well-defined "circle of competence." The idea is not just intellectual. It's psychological. If you know what's inside your circle—what industries you understand, what business models you trust—you don't waste energy on everything else. You skip 99% of headlines and focus on the 1% that matter to *your strategy*. That is not constraint. That is freedom with shape.

And yet, no structure is complete without feedback. Once you begin making decisions within your filtered environment, *track your own responses*. Don't just analyse your portfolio's performance—analyse your behaviour. When did you hesitate? What choices drained your energy? Which ones felt clear and repeatable? This meta-cognition—thinking about your own thinking—is what transforms tactics into philosophy. Over time, you'll notice patterns. You'll see that certain sources of input always leave you more confused than informed. You'll learn which decisions need more data and which need more reflection. You'll begin to build *judgement*, which is the rarest asset in investing.

Importantly, you'll also begin to trust yourself. One of the hidden dangers of chronic choice is the erosion of self-trust. If every decision feels equally fraught, and the outcomes are always uncertain, it's easy to internalise a subtle message: *maybe I'm just not good at this.* But the truth is, no one is "good" at investing by default. What sets long-term investors apart is not their innate foresight—it's their ability to *systematically reduce the number of decisions they need to get right.* They design environments that make their strengths easier to express and their weaknesses less likely to sabotage them.

Ultimately, the paradox of choice teaches us a critical investing principle: success is not about seeing every possibility. It is about *curating the possibilities that match your principles, goals, and temperament.* Your job as an investor is not to optimise every trade. It is to create a durable framework within which good decisions can repeat. Decision fatigue isn't a failing. It's a signal. It tells you that your environment is asking too much of your cognitive resources—and it invites you to respond not with more force, but with better structure.

The goal, then, is not to eliminate choice, but to *elevate decision quality by reducing decision volume.* You cannot control the market. But you can control the architecture of your own process—the information you allow in, the routines you commit to, the boundaries you enforce. That architecture becomes your edge. Not because it guarantees perfect outcomes, but because it *preserves clarity* in a world designed to fragment it.

Automating What You Can, Intending What You Must

If you had to make a conscious decision every morning to brush your teeth, chances are, you'd occasionally forget. But because it's a habit embedded in a system—triggered by routine, executed without debate—you do it consistently, even when distracted. The same principle applies to investing. The more you can remove unnecessary friction from essential behaviours, the more consistently those behaviours occur. This is the case for automation—not as a trendy tech solution, but as a psychological tool. *Automation exists not to replace intelligence, but to preserve it for when it's most needed.*

One of the most common misconceptions among new investors is that each financial action must be approached with fresh deliberation. They assume that every deposit, every trade, every review must be consciously initiated, manually executed, and constantly reassessed. While admirable in intent, this approach is cognitively unsustainable. Decision fatigue sets in quickly. Even highly motivated individuals cannot maintain daily engagement at a high quality without compromising consistency or clarity. Automation solves this—not by removing human judgement, but by *elevating its role.* It offloads repeatable, low-variance tasks so that attention can be focused where judgement truly adds value: on what to buy, why to own it, and when to exit.

Begin with the most foundational building block: capital contribution. Your investment results, especially early on, are disproportionately shaped not by market returns, but by how much you save and how consistently you invest. Automating contributions from your primary income source to your brokerage account ensures that this foundational step is never left to emotional discretion or monthly guesswork. Set it up once—weekly, bi-weekly, or monthly—and it becomes a background process, like pension withholding or rent payment. Over time, this rhythm builds both wealth and identity. *You stop thinking of investing as an act of willpower and start seeing it as part of your behavioural infrastructure.*

But automation does not end at contribution. Many brokerages now allow you to set up recurring investments into specific securities—particularly index funds and ETFs. This can be powerful, especially for long-term, diversified holdings. It protects you from market timing errors and ensures that you participate in the market's compounding effects regardless of short-term volatility. The psychological benefit is equally important: by making your investing process predictable, you reduce stress and reduce the temptation to tinker unnecessarily.

However, the temptation to over-automate is real. Not everything in investing *should* be set on autopilot. Certain decisions demand reflection, especially those tied to ownership and exit. Stock selection—at least for individual equities—is a fundamentally human act. It requires understanding the business, evaluating its strategy, judging the integrity of management, and placing that analysis within the broader context of your financial goals and temperament. No algorithm can fully encode this complexity. It must be done with deliberation and care. *Automation may get your capital into the market—but only intention ensures it's placed in alignment with your convictions.*

This creates a necessary bifurcation in your investing architecture. Automate *contributions and structural behaviours*. Intend *allocations and decisions of significance*. This division is not a contradiction—it's a design principle. It reflects the nature of the mind: you are most likely to succeed when you combine system-driven reliability with strategically deployed attention.

Consider the problem of rebalancing. It's the periodic process of adjusting your portfolio back to its intended asset allocation. It is, in principle, a mechanical task. But in practice, it can be emotionally charged—especially after periods of extreme volatility. If stocks have surged, reducing exposure feels like missing out. If equities have plunged, buying more feels reckless. This is precisely when automation can help. By scheduling quarterly or semi-annual rebalancing reminders and setting clear rebalancing rules in advance—such as tolerances for deviation or predefined thresholds—you reduce emotional interference. The decision still involves human input, but it's guided by a pre-committed framework. *Pre-commitment, when paired with automation, creates resilience.*

Another domain where automation helps is behavioural correction. Suppose you find that you're prone to checking your portfolio too frequently, leading to stress and reactive decisions. You can automate friction into your process: remove price alerts, log out of your app after trades, restrict trading hours via app permissions, or create a personal cooling-off rule—e.g., no trading allowed within 48 hours of a major news event. These are not limitations. They are self-imposed guardrails. *Smart automation doesn't just accelerate action—it can strategically slow you down.*

At the same time, intention must remain active when it comes to your investing principles. Why do you own what you own? What is the role of each asset in your portfolio? What scenarios would cause you to exit a position? These questions cannot be automated. They require writing, reflection, and revision. A useful exercise is to create an "investment decision memo" for each significant purchase. Not a spreadsheet or a checklist, but a brief narrative: Why am I buying this? What do I understand about the company or fund? What would make me revisit this decision? These memos are invaluable when fear or hype strikes. They become a touchstone when your memory of the original rationale is blurred by the passage of time or by market chaos.

Exit decisions, in particular, demand human presence. Selling is arguably harder than buying. It involves not only financial implications but ego, regret, opportunity cost, and counterfactual thinking. When do you admit that a stock no longer fits your thesis? When do you take profits without anchoring to arbitrary price targets? There is no formula for this, but there *is* a discipline: define your sell conditions in advance, document your reasoning, and resist the urge to react impulsively to price movement alone. Automation has no answer here—but your prior reflection does.

The deeper point here is about *energy allocation.* You have a finite amount of mental bandwidth to apply to your investing life. If you spend it all on low-value, repetitive decisions—when to transfer funds, what amount to invest this month, which stocks are "trending"—you leave little left for the decisions that actually matter.

But if you automate what can be reliably delegated to systems, and protect your energy for the moments that demand strategic attention, you create a more sustainable practice. You reduce the chances of burnout. You protect your judgement from erosion. You build *consistency without complacency*.

There is also a moral and philosophical dimension to this approach. Automated investing often assumes a kind of passive obedience to the market's rhythm. But intention asks: what am I aligning myself with? What kind of businesses do I want to own? What does responsible capital stewardship look like for me? These are not questions a robo-advisor can answer. Nor should they be. They are the essence of ownership. Automation is powerful—but it must *serve* your values, not replace them.

At its best, automation is a scaffold. It holds your system in place while your mind attends to the deeper work of alignment, learning, and calibration. It is not the goal. It is the support. The purpose is not to remove all effort from investing, but to *direct effort where it counts*. Knowing when to let systems run and when to step in with judgement is one of the highest forms of financial maturity. It reflects a shift from reaction to design—from improvisation to structure.

Investing is not an intellectual contest. It is a behavioural one. The most successful investors are not the ones with the most information, but the ones with the most effective architecture for decision-making. Automation is not about shortcuts. It's about *respecting your limited time, energy, and attention*—and using them with care.

So automate what you can: transfers, contributions, reminders, rebalancing thresholds, behavioural guardrails. But intend what you must: allocation, asset selection, risk management, exits, principles. This isn't a compromise between technology and thought. It is their optimal combination. The future of investing belongs not to those who react fastest, but to those who act *with clarity*. And clarity begins when you no longer waste attention on what systems can do for you—because you've preserved it for what only you can do well.

You Are Not Your Portfolio, But It Reflects You

If you want to understand someone's values, don't ask what they say—look at how they allocate their time, energy, and capital. Investing, stripped of abstraction, is a practical expression of belief. Your portfolio may not define you, but it does *reflect* you: how you see the world, what you believe is worth building, and what kind of future you're implicitly funding. Yet too often, portfolios are assembled reactively—bits of advice, articles, headlines, and trends stitched together without coherence. What emerges is not a strategy, but a scattered response to noise. The antidote to this fragmentation is intentionality. And the clearest articulation of that intent is your *Personal Investment Manifesto.*

A manifesto is not a slogan. It is a considered statement of vision and practice—personal, principled, and revisable over time. It is not meant to impress others, but to anchor *you.* When written properly, it becomes your compass in times of chaos and a filter in times of temptation. It tells you what to ignore, what to focus on, and what to return to when you feel lost in volatility. It is, at its core, a declaration of clarity.

Before you can write one, however, you must confront a difficult truth: most portfolios are a mirror of unexamined habits. Some reflect fear—an overconcentration in cash or overly conservative allocations that reveal a deep aversion to risk. Others reflect fantasy—hyper-aggressive bets on speculative assets with no relationship to one's actual time horizon or goals. Many reflect social influence—purchases made under the sway of groupthink, media hype, or peer imitation. These portfolios don't lie, even if their owners are unaware of the story they're telling. They reveal what is driving the investor at a deeper level: insecurity, mimicry, wishful thinking, avoidance. *To become a thoughtful investor, you must be willing to see this mirror clearly—and not flinch.*

This doesn't mean that your portfolio must be flawless. It means that it must be *honest.* It should correspond to who you are, where you are in life, and where you want to be—not in idealistic terms, but in practical, behaviourally realistic terms. If you're 32, living in a high-cost city, building a family, and running a freelance career with inconsistent income, your portfolio should not look like that of a 55-year-old executive with stable cash flow and institutional backing. But this is precisely what happens when people invest without introspection. They adopt generic models or mimic high-profile investors without calibrating to their own context.

This is where writing your manifesto begins—not with markets, but with *you.* Who are you when it comes to money? What are your non-negotiables? What kind of financial life do you want to create? What role should investing play within that life—growth, income, optionality, contribution? What kind of volatility are you willing to endure, and what kind are you not? What are you optimising for—maximum returns, peace of mind, flexibility, legacy? These questions do not have objectively correct answers. They have *your* answers. The act of clarifying them is itself transformative.

The process of writing a Personal Investment Manifesto should be uncomfortable. If it feels like a motivational listicle, you're doing it wrong. It should force confrontation with competing priorities. For instance, you might realise that you value both financial independence and a sense of stewardship—but that your recent trading behaviour reflects neither. You might believe in supporting sustainable companies, but own positions in firms whose practices you'd be unwilling to defend in conversation. These tensions are not failures. They are signals. They show you where your investing identity is still being formed—and where attention is needed.

The manifesto should also distinguish between principle and tactic. "I will invest in companies I understand" is a principle. "I will buy shares in XYZ tech company next week" is a tactic. The former guides the latter. Too often, investors mistake tactics for strategy and end up in a cycle of short-term responsiveness. But a manifesto lives above the tactical level. It clarifies your orientation: what kind of investor you're trying to be, what you will and won't engage with, and how you will define progress.

One of the most powerful roles a manifesto plays is during market stress. When volatility strikes—whether through a global event, a recession, or a single bad earnings report—it's tempting to throw out every plan and react. But a manifesto written during calm, grounded in long-term thinking, gives you something to return to. It might remind you: "My investment horizon is 20 years, and this decline does not alter the underlying thesis of the businesses I own." Or: "I expect at least one 30% drawdown every decade. This is part of the game, not an exception." These are not platitudes. They are behavioural inoculations—predefined scripts for staying rational when your nervous system is screaming for action.

Moreover, your manifesto can help you draw boundaries—not just in what you invest in, but in how you engage. For example, it might include statements such as: "I will only evaluate portfolio performance quarterly, not daily." Or: "I do not check my brokerage account during market open hours unless I have a planned reason." These micro-rules are not constraints—they are structure. They protect you from your own worst impulses by giving your best self the final word.

Your manifesto may also evolve to include elements of ethical alignment. As investing becomes more accessible, so too does the opportunity to align capital with conscience. You may choose to avoid industries that conflict with your values or to direct a portion of your investments toward businesses solving real societal problems. But these choices should not be made reactively. They should emerge from reflection. What does responsible investing mean to you? How do you weigh short-term profit against long-term impact? How much of your portfolio, if any, do you want to dedicate to purpose-driven ventures? These are not trivial additions. They define the moral texture of your investing practice.

There's also the question of identity. Too often, people conflate their net worth with their self-worth. A bad quarter feels like a personal failure. A market rally brings undeserved pride. This is why the phrase "You are not your portfolio" is essential. Your value is not determined by your returns. But *your portfolio does reflect you*—your discipline, your thoughtfulness, your capacity for delayed gratification. It is a record of your behaviour under uncertainty. It won't always be flattering, but it will always be instructive. The goal is not to judge it, but to learn from it.

Writing your manifesto should be an iterative process. Set aside time. Write freely. Revisit it quarterly. See how your convictions evolve. You may find that you become more tolerant of volatility, or less interested in active selection. You may discover new insights into what money means to you—not just as a resource, but as a signal of trust, freedom, or even anxiety. Document these shifts. They are not detours. They are the evolution of a thinking investor.

A well-written manifesto is not long. It is precise. It may be no more than one page. But within that page, it should reflect thought, integrity, and perspective. It should answer, in clear terms: *What do I believe about investing? What do I value? What am I building? And what behaviour do I commit to—regardless of external conditions?* When markets are stable, it will feel like a quiet guide. When markets are chaotic, it will feel like a lifeline.

Ultimately, your manifesto is a commitment—not to performance, but to process. Not to outcomes, but to character. Investing is not an isolated skill. It is part of a life. And the more clearly you understand who you are and what you stand for, the more coherently your capital will move in alignment. You are not your portfolio. But your portfolio, like a journal or a mirror, will always be reflecting something back to you. The question is: do you like what you see—and if not, what will you write into it next?

Chapter 3
Buying Your First Stock—A Ceremony, Not a Bet

There is a particular gravity to doing something for the first time. Firsts mark thresholds—between idea and action, observation and participation, preparation and identity. Buying your first stock is far more than an economic decision; it is a psychological initiation. In that moment, you move from spectator to owner, from someone who reads about markets to someone who steps in with skin in the game. The shift is subtle, yet profound. No simulator, no paper portfolio, can replicate it. Until real capital is at stake—until you see it fluctuate in real time, tugging at your attention and shaping your beliefs—you haven't truly begun investing. You've only rehearsed.

That initial trade is often accompanied by anxiety, not merely because of financial stakes, but because it represents a deeper shift in identity. For many, it is the first conscious act of ownership in their adult financial life. Up to that point, money has largely been about earning, spending, perhaps saving. Investing introduces a new verb: building. And with that verb comes responsibility. Suddenly, you are not tracking prices or following headlines; you are a participant in a living, evolving enterprise. Your stake can rise—or fall. That ambiguity unsettles many, not because the risk is unknowable, but because the psychological framework is unfamiliar.

Compounding this unease is the pervasive notion that there exists a "right" answer—a magical alignment of timing and insight that will validate your competence. This belief is unnecessary and counterproductive. It fosters what psychologists call analysis paralysis: the fear of a suboptimal choice freezes action entirely. Ironically, in pursuit of perfection, many never step in at all, thereby missing the central lesson: clarity is forged through engagement, not endless deliberation.

This chapter seeks to dissolve that paralysis, not with promises of a perfect formula, but by reframing the act of buying your first stock as a deliberate rite of passage. Outperformance on the first trade is irrelevant. Impressing anyone else is irrelevant. What matters is stepping in with thoughtfulness, curiosity, and a commitment to learning—qualities infinitely more valuable than the hottest tip or trend.

To guide this, you are introduced to a practical, intellectually disciplined framework: the First Stock Filter. It is minimalist yet robust, designed to convert overwhelm into intentionality. No exotic metrics, no insider tools—just four essential questions: Do you understand the business? Does it have a sustainable advantage? Are its earnings reasonably predictable? Is the price justified by available information? Familiar concepts, often overlooked amid noise, speculation, or haste, yet foundational to disciplined investing.

Clarity on paper, however, must eventually meet reality. Many begin with businesses they already know: products they use, services they trust, brands they respect. These familiar companies are not automatic recommendations, but they offer a gateway. Familiarity fosters understanding, and understanding mitigates emotional overreaction. Yet even then, one must shift from consumer to investor lens. Ask: What is the company's competitive moat? How does it generate revenue? Is customer loyalty enduring or ephemeral? What are its pricing dynamics and cash flow cycles? Loving a brand is insufficient; one must comprehend and value the business model itself.

What follows the purchase is as important as the act itself. Many imagine that clicking "buy" completes the process. In truth, it is the beginning of a relationship—between you and the company, between you and the market, and most critically, between you and your evolving investing self. Enter the Stock Memory Journal: a deceptively simple, profoundly transformative practice. Record, in your own words, why you purchased, what you understood at the time, what you expected, and the conditions that would prompt reconsideration. This record becomes an anchor, tracking cognitive and emotional patterns as volatility inevitably arrives.

Too few investors integrate this reflective layer. Charts, earnings reports, and ratios are scrutinised, yet their own minds—the true drivers of long-term outcomes—are neglected. Ownership is a test of internal systems: what emotions does it provoke? How do you respond to uncertainty? What narratives arise as prices move? These invisible, yet critical, dimensions of competence surface the instant you shift from observer to participant.

It bears repeating: buying your first stock is neither a gamble nor a game. It is a ceremony—a conscious entry into capital stewardship. It is your first act of economic agency, a vote of belief in a business and, by extension, in your capacity to contribute to long-term value creation. That belief should be informed, tested, challenged—but also affirmed through thoughtful action.

This chapter exists to ease that affirmation. You will explore the psychology of first-time investing: the feel of fear, navigating it, and discerning signal from noise. Tools and frameworks simplify decisions without reducing rigor. You'll learn to balance intuition with evidence, familiarity with analysis, confidence with humility. Most crucially, you will see that this act—your first investment—is not isolated, but the inception of a deliberate, values-based practice.

As you proceed, reflect not only on what stock to purchase, but on the kind of investor you are becoming. What you buy matters, but how, why, and under what framework you buy matters far more. Let this be not a leap of faith, but a step of intention. Not a test of luck, but a marker of evolution. Once you own a stock, you are no longer on the sidelines. You are in the arena—and that transition is worth approaching deliberately.

Why 'Getting In' Is More Emotional Than Technical:

There's a moment—brief, often silent—when your finger hovers over the "Buy" button. The decision has been made in theory. The research is done. The brokerage account is funded. But still, you hesitate. Why? Not because you doubt the mechanics, but because something deeper is happening: this isn't just a financial transaction. It's a psychological crossing. You are stepping into ownership. And for most new investors, that first act of getting in isn't defined by spreadsheets or strategy—it's defined by emotion.

Most discussions about investing start with metrics: price-to-earnings ratios, dividend yields, balance sheets. These are important, but they are not the first hurdle. The first hurdle is *yourself*. The fear of being wrong. The exposure of being visible—to yourself, if not to others. The subtle but powerful shift in identity that comes from moving out of analysis and into action. Until this point, you've had the luxury of detachment. You've read books, studied charts, maybe even back-tested ideas. But once you place that order, you're no longer theorising. You're committing. And that commitment feels riskier than it looks on paper.

This fear isn't irrational. It's ancestral. Humans have always been wired to avoid uncertainty, especially where loss is involved. Behavioural economists call it *loss aversion*—the well-documented tendency to feel the pain of a loss more intensely than the pleasure of a gain. When you make your first investment, you are, in effect, confronting this evolutionary bias. You are choosing to override your default programming and embrace the possibility of discomfort for the sake of long-term growth. That's not trivial. It's a form of psychological resistance training.

But there's more at stake than fear alone. What's also at play is identity disruption. Until now, your financial self may have been defined primarily as a saver, spender, or perhaps a cautious planner. Investing reconfigures that identity. It forces you to think in terms of ownership, volatility, and long-term consequence. It makes you an active participant in the economy, rather than a passive observer. This reframing can be invigorating—but also destabilising. Who are you when you own a company? What kind of responsibility comes with that? And what does it say about you if that investment falters?

This is precisely why the act of getting in should not be treated casually. It deserves to be recognised as a moment of transformation. Think of it as a ceremonial threshold—the point at which your intentions become tangible. You're not just buying a ticker symbol. You're entering into a relationship with a business, exposing yourself to the psychology of markets, and—most significantly—confronting the reality that financial outcomes are always uncertain, regardless of preparation.

The financial industry tends to downplay this inner terrain. It prefers to sell systems, tools, and tactical advice—things that can be packaged, quantified, and marketed. But if you've ever spoken to seasoned investors, they rarely attribute their longevity to secret formulas. More often, they talk about temperament. About learning to live with discomfort. About knowing when not to act. These are emotional competencies, not technical skills. And they begin to develop only once you step into ownership.

For many first-time investors, the pressure to "get it right" on the first trade is paralysing. This expectation is not only unnecessary; it's toxic. It frames investing as a test of correctness rather than a process of learning. But mastery doesn't emerge from a flawless first choice. It emerges from engagement, reflection, and adaptation. You learn more from owning one imperfectly timed stock than from analysing a hundred with no money on the line. *Skin in the game clarifies thinking.* It sharpens your attention, accelerates your education, and, most importantly, reveals your behavioural tendencies in a way that paper portfolios never could.

Consider this: you could read a thousand pages on investing theory, but nothing will prepare you for the visceral experience of watching your investment decline 10% the day after you buy it. Or the euphoria that comes from a surprise rally. Or the second-guessing that sets in when others are making money in things you don't own. These emotional states are not bugs in the system—they *are* the system. Markets are not just engines of capital allocation; they are mirrors of collective psychology. And when you invest, you become part of that psychological loop.

The question, then, is how to enter with care—how to navigate the emotional significance of getting in without being consumed by it. The answer lies in reframing the act not as a bet, but as a step into alignment. You're not trying to beat the market. You're trying to become the kind of person who acts with clarity, intention, and resilience. That means defining success not by short-term performance, but by behavioural integrity. Did you follow your process? Did you act on principles rather than impulses? Did you learn something meaningful about yourself and the business you bought into?

Some might argue that emotion has no place in investing—that the goal is to remain coldly rational. But this is both unrealistic and unwise. Emotion is not the enemy. *Unexamined* emotion is. The goal is not to suppress feeling, but to be aware of it, to incorporate it into your practice without letting it drive your decisions. And this is why your first investment is so valuable: it brings those emotions to the surface. It gives you a chance to observe your own psychology in action. That observation is the beginning of wisdom.

A powerful exercise at this stage is to write down your thoughts immediately before and after placing your first trade. What did you expect to feel? What did you actually feel? What stories did your mind create—about the company, about the outcome, about yourself? These notes will become more valuable over time than any chart or spreadsheet. They are a record of your inner investor—raw, evolving, and real. Over time, you'll be able to see how your mindset shifts, where your biases show up, and how your sense of self changes as your experience grows.

It's also important to place this first step in a wider context. Buying your first stock doesn't mean you now need to build a full portfolio overnight. You're not obligated to become an expert in all sectors or to keep up with every market trend. You don't need to know everything. You need to *start*—with one thoughtful, intentional move. Then observe. Reflect. And begin again, a little more informed. This is how sustainable investing competence is built—not in surges of enthusiasm, but in steady iterations.

Finally, let's acknowledge that fear never fully disappears. Even veteran investors feel it—especially when the stakes are high. What changes over time is not the absence of emotion, but the expansion of perspective. The first time you invest, a 5% dip feels like a catastrophe. The tenth time, it feels like an inconvenience. The hundredth time, it may feel like an opportunity. This evolution can't be downloaded. It must be lived. And it starts with that first act of stepping in—not perfectly, but *deliberately*.

Getting in is more emotional than technical because it touches the very architecture of who you are: your beliefs, your fears, your capacity to act in the face of uncertainty. That's what makes it powerful. And that's why it matters. If you understand this, you won't just become an investor in markets. You'll become an investor in your own growth. And that is the real return you're compounding from the moment you begin.

"Analysis Paralysis and the Search for the 'Perfect' Pick":

The idea of buying a single share of stock can ignite an unexpected cascade of indecision. For a new investor, the sheer magnitude of options—thousands of public companies, each with its own history, numbers, and story—can produce not confidence, but paralysis. It is easy to assume that the challenge lies in a lack of information. But more often, the true obstacle is too much of it. Every article, analyst opinion, Reddit thread, and chart becomes another voice in an overcrowded mental auditorium, all shouting different things. And so, the first-time investor finds themselves frozen—not because the risk is overwhelming, but because the need to make the *perfect* decision becomes an emotional burden.

Perfection is not just the enemy of progress—it's the architect of delay. It disguises itself as discipline, as intellectual rigour, as prudence. But its effect is stasis. And in investing, stasis costs money—not just in missed returns, but in the erosion of learning that only real engagement produces. The most painful form of inaction is not the kind that comes from fear, but the kind that dresses up as due diligence long past its usefulness.

This is why a simplified framework—anchored in clarity rather than complexity—is essential. A new investor does not need to master discounted cash flow models or study sector rotation theory before buying their first stock. They need a lens through which to filter the noise, a small set of principles that can be trusted to point in the direction of quality without claiming predictive perfection. Enter the *First Stock Filter*—a four-part decision compass that prioritises businesses that are easy to understand, fundamentally sound, and reasonably priced. These criteria will not guarantee success, but they will give your first investment something far more powerful: a foundation of intention.

The first element of this filter is *Understandable Business*. If you can't explain what a company does, how it makes money, and what threatens its ability to continue doing so, you are not ready to invest in it. This may sound obvious, but too often beginners are lured into complexity under the assumption that sophistication equals opportunity. It does not. Legendary investors from Peter Lynch to Warren Buffett have long emphasised the virtue of staying within one's circle of competence. This is not a limitation—it is a strength. When you begin with companies whose services or products you use, interact with, or observe regularly, you are more likely to understand the nature of their business model and the realism of their growth potential. Complexity can wait. Start with clarity.

Second, seek a *Sustainable Advantage*. This refers to what Warren Buffett famously called the company's "economic moat"—something that protects it from competition. It could be brand loyalty (as with Apple), cost leadership (as with Walmart), proprietary technology (as with Nvidia), or network effects (as with Visa or Meta). The critical question is not just whether the company is successful now, but whether it has some structural reason to remain successful despite inevitable competition. Without such an advantage, today's profits are tomorrow's margin erosion. The moat doesn't have to be enormous, but it must be identifiable and durable.

The third component is *Predictable Earnings*. This is not about precision forecasting. No one can reliably predict quarterly results, and trying to do so often leads to short-term thinking. Rather, this principle is about pattern recognition. Is the company's revenue relatively stable or wildly cyclical? Does its profitability fluctuate violently with commodity prices, or does it have a repeatable, resilient earnings base? A business with highly volatile earnings may not be inappropriate—but it requires a temperament and time horizon that can tolerate sharp ups and downs. For most first-time investors, stable and modestly growing earnings provide the psychological safety to remain invested, especially during market dips.

Finally, the filter includes *Reasonable Price*. This is where many new investors stumble. Valuation is both an art and a science, and it can be intimidating. But you do not need to identify "the cheapest stock on the market" to avoid overpaying. What you need is context. Compare the company's current price-to-earnings (P/E) ratio with its own historical average, its industry peers, and its growth rate. Avoid companies with valuations that imply perfection—because when expectations are sky-high, even good news can disappoint. The goal is not to find the absolute bargain, but to avoid paying for hype. If the business is understandable, has a moat, and delivers consistent earnings, then paying a fair (not discounted) price can still lead to strong long-term returns.

What this framework does is eliminate the illusion that there is such a thing as the "perfect" first stock. There isn't. Markets are forward-looking, businesses evolve, and what appears to be an excellent pick today may lag behind tomorrow. But this uncertainty should not paralyse you—it should sober you. Perfection is not a prerequisite for participation. The aim is not to be right in the short term, but to be reasonable over the long term. And reason starts with a simple, consistent lens for evaluating opportunities.

Of course, this begs the question: if you follow this filter and still hesitate, what's stopping you? Often, the paralysis persists not because the process is unclear, but because the emotional stakes feel high. You worry that a bad first choice will brand you as an incompetent investor. But this is a false belief. Investing is not a single test of judgment. It is a cumulative practice. The first pick is not a verdict—it is a data point. What matters most is *not* whether it outperforms, but whether it teaches. If it does, then it was the right first pick, regardless of return.

It's also worth examining how culture compounds this paralysis. We are conditioned to believe that good decisions are those that lead to good outcomes. But in investing, this is often not the case. A good decision can lead to a poor short-term result due to randomness or macro conditions. Likewise, a bad decision can sometimes be rewarded purely by luck. This disconnection between process and outcome makes investing uniquely vulnerable to second-guessing. But the antidote is process discipline. If your choice was filtered through a framework rooted in clarity and logic, then the process was sound. And that's what builds durable confidence—not winning trades, but consistent reasoning.

To illustrate this, consider a case study from a first-time investor who bought shares of McDonald's—not because of hype, but because they understood the business model, recognised the brand strength, appreciated the consistency of earnings, and found the price reasonable based on past performance. For the first six months, the stock barely moved. Then it declined slightly. The investor felt tempted to sell. But they revisited their rationale and remembered that fast food is a defensive sector, with long-term demand stability. Over the next 18 months, the company beat earnings expectations, expanded its app-based sales channel, and outperformed the broader market. The key lesson? It wasn't timing or insight that won—it was patience rooted in clarity.

Contrast this with someone who fixated on finding the *next big tech winner*, scanning hundreds of small-cap names, poring over obscure metrics, only to buy into a speculative biotech firm they didn't fully understand. The price doubled in three weeks—then halved. The investor panicked, sold at a loss, and walked away disillusioned. The issue was not the volatility. It was the absence of process. The decision was based on hope, not understanding. And hope, in investing, is not a strategy—it's a liability.

What these examples underscore is the importance of framing your first investment not as a test of intelligence, but as a practice in clarity. By anchoring your decision to four foundational ideas—*understandable business, sustainable advantage, predictable earnings, reasonable price*—you give yourself structure, not guarantees. But structure is enough. It transforms the chaotic buffet of options into a thoughtful shortlist. It quiets the noise, sharpens your thinking, and reduces the cognitive overload that often masquerades as wisdom.

Ultimately, the path to investing maturity does not begin with brilliance. It begins with *motion.* Thoughtful, intentional motion. You will never have all the data. You will never eliminate all doubt. But you can eliminate the illusion that more analysis will save you from uncertainty. It won't. At some point, you must choose. And when you do, make it a choice grounded in clarity—not perfection. Because clarity, unlike perfection, compounds.

"From Brands You Love to Businesses You Understand":

Many new investors begin their journey with a simple, seemingly intuitive idea: invest in what you know. It's a principle popularised by legendary fund manager Peter Lynch, who famously encouraged individuals to start with the companies they see, use, and trust in daily life. On the surface, this advice appears almost too obvious.

You drink Starbucks, use an iPhone, shop on Amazon, wear Nike trainers—why not own a piece of the companies behind them? This familiarity breeds confidence, and confidence makes it easier to take the first step into the market. But while brand familiarity may be a good entry point, it is not an endpoint. Knowing a logo is not the same as understanding a business. The leap from consumer to investor requires a shift in thinking—from surface recognition to structural curiosity.

A strong brand does not guarantee a strong business. The distinction is subtle but critical. As a consumer, you engage with products through experience, convenience, design, and emotional connection. As an investor, you must interrogate how that experience translates into revenue, margins, capital efficiency, and long-term viability. That transformation begins by looking beyond the packaging. When you admire a company, ask: how does this company make money, how defensible is that stream of income, and how disciplined is the company in reinvesting its profits?

Consider Apple. Millions of people adore its products. But from an investor's perspective, Apple is not just a hardware company—it is a cash-generation machine with a vast services ecosystem, high customer retention, and enviable pricing power. Its gross margins are not simply the result of technological excellence, but of supply chain mastery, brand loyalty, and vertical integration. An Apple enthusiast may understand why the iPhone is delightful to use. But an Apple investor must understand why customers upgrade regularly, why the company has resisted commoditisation, and how it turns hardware sales into recurring services revenue. In other words, *the product is the doorway; the business model is the architecture behind it.*

This principle also applies in reverse. Some businesses with lacklustre brand appeal may be exceptional investments. Take waste management. It is not glamorous, nor does it feature in social media conversations or consumer wishlists. But companies like Waste

Management Inc. in the United States have delivered stable returns for years due to regulatory moats, predictable cash flows, and limited competition. Their strength lies in boring reliability, not emotional resonance. Investing only in companies you emotionally admire risks ignoring the structural realities that drive sustainable profitability.

This is where the practice of *deepening your curiosity* becomes essential. Once a company captures your attention—through a product, service, or brand—use that attention as a launching pad. Peel back the layers. How many revenue streams does it have? Is it dependent on one flagship product or diversified across geographies and customer segments? Does it face meaningful threats from regulation, changing technology, or consumer preferences? A surface-level opinion may suffice at dinner parties, but investing demands depth. It is only through understanding the operational backbone that you gain the conviction to hold through volatility and the insight to interpret price movements in context.

Customer loyalty is another area worth careful study. Brand affinity and customer stickiness are not the same. A customer may love a product but be willing to switch the moment a cheaper or trendier option appears. Others may be locked into an ecosystem by design—whether through subscriptions, proprietary technology, or logistical convenience. For instance, Adobe users often stay not because the brand is beloved, but because switching costs are high and workflows are entrenched. Similarly, Amazon Prime is less about affection than about frictionless logistics and bundled value. The underlying lesson: *loyalty is not always emotional—it is often functional.* Understanding that nuance can sharpen your assessment of a company's defensibility.

Another key factor is pricing power—the ability of a business to raise prices without losing customers. This is one of the most overlooked and yet most telling indicators of a company's competitive strength. Brands you love might feel premium to you, but are they truly insulated from price sensitivity? Netflix is a useful example. As it raised prices over the years, its subscriber base initially remained resilient. But eventually, consumers began to balk, prompting churn and the exploration of ad-supported models. Contrast this with luxury brands like Hermès, which routinely raise prices and continue to grow demand. *Liking a product is not proof of pricing power—evidence lies in how customers behave, not how they feel.*

Once you begin to develop this business-focused lens, your portfolio starts to shift. You no longer chase logos or trending names—you investigate moats, balance sheets, capital allocation discipline, and shareholder alignment. You read earnings calls, not just headlines. And when the market panics, you are less likely to sell, because you are anchored in comprehension, not hype.

This shift also transforms how you think about diversification. It's easy to believe that investing in Apple, Nike, Starbucks, and Netflix provides variety—they come from different industries, after all. But they may be driven by similar economic forces: discretionary consumer spending, brand perception, and U.S.-centric demand. When a recession hits or consumer sentiment falters, these companies may decline in unison. A more mature approach recognises the difference between superficial variety and *true business model diversification*—owning companies with different revenue cycles, customer bases, regulatory exposures, and economic sensitivities.

That level of nuance requires effort, but the effort pays dividends—in confidence, in clarity, and in resilience. When your investment decisions are rooted in curiosity, you are no longer at the mercy of market moods. You become less vulnerable to media noise, guru forecasts, or short-term price swings. You build what might be called *conviction literacy*—the ability to think independently, hold steadily, and adjust rationally.

To cultivate this mindset, one practice stands out: keep an investor's journal. Every time a company catches your attention, write down why. Then take it further. Map out its revenue drivers, read its most recent investor presentation, identify competitors, and study its last three years of financials. Note how its stock has behaved in past market drawdowns. Ask yourself what it would take for you to no longer want to hold it. This habit not only sharpens your judgement but builds a personal database of understanding that compounds over time.

From brands you love to businesses you understand—this is not just a slogan. It is a developmental arc. It marks the movement from being a passive consumer of financial content to an active thinker in the world of capital. It teaches you to distinguish signal from noise, quality from familiarity, and strategy from sentiment. It anchors your portfolio not in admiration, but in analysis.

Most importantly, it shifts the centre of gravity in your investing practice. Instead of asking "What stock should I buy?" you begin to ask, "What do I understand well enough to own with conviction?" That shift—from chasing answers to crafting your own questions—is what elevates you from beginner to practitioner. Not because you know more facts, but because you've built a way of thinking that outlasts the headlines. That is what investing, at its most meaningful level, demands—not perfection, but pattern recognition born of curiosity, rigour, and clarity.

"The Day After: What to Do Once You Own Something":

Buying a stock may feel like the finish line—months of research distilled into a single button press. Yet in truth, that moment marks the beginning of a much more consequential phase: *ownership*. The day after you buy your first share is where investing stops being a hypothetical exercise and becomes a lived psychological reality. Now, your money is in motion. Now, you're exposed. Now, you're vulnerable to yourself. What you do next—how you think, how you feel, how you respond to noise—will shape not just your returns, but your entire evolution as an investor.

The first common mistake new investors make post-purchase is to confuse price movement with portfolio performance. It's a natural impulse. You refresh the trading app. You check the ticker. You experience a brief rush when the price ticks up and a subtle dread when it dips. This feedback loop is as addictive as it is misleading. It trains you to react, not reflect. But markets don't reward reactivity—they reward patience informed by insight. The antidote to this behavioural trap lies not in ignoring the market altogether, but in creating a structured way to observe both your investment and your internal response to it. That's where the *Stock Memory Journal* becomes invaluable.

A Stock Memory Journal is not a trading log. It is not about recording buy and sell prices. It is a disciplined habit designed to capture your thinking—before, during, and after you own a stock. Its purpose is threefold: to anchor your decisions in clarity, to track the evolution of your convictions, and to provide a space for cooling psychological volatility. The discipline of writing allows you to translate emotional noise into cognitive structure. It's where intuition meets evidence. And over time, it becomes your most personalised source of investing insight.

Begin by documenting your original thesis: *Why did you buy this company?* Not in abstract terms, but with specificity. What did you understand about its business model, its competitive edge, its earnings quality, or its capital discipline? What metrics or indicators gave you confidence? What risks did you acknowledge but accept? Writing this down creates a timestamped snapshot of your logic at the moment of action—a touchstone to return to when markets become unstable or your resolve wavers. It allows you to later distinguish between justified concern and emotional reaction.

This reflection also immunises you against the most corrosive investing impulse: *panic-selling.* Without a documented thesis, the mind invents new narratives when prices fall. A 15% drop no longer reflects market turbulence—it suddenly becomes a referendum on your intelligence. You second-guess your choice. You worry about further loss. You exit at the wrong time for the wrong reason. But if you can revisit your original thinking and ask whether the underlying business has changed—rather than reacting to the price—you reclaim perspective. Panic arises when we confuse movement with meaning. Journaling helps you separate the two.

The second key component of post-purchase behaviour is setting an intentional *holding period.* This is not a rigid rule but a conscious commitment. It's your personal buffer against short-term noise. The moment you own a stock, you are tempted to become its babysitter. You check its status daily. You interpret every headline as a potential threat. But most businesses do not evolve meaningfully in a single day or week. Their quarterly performance, strategic decisions, and competitive dynamics play out across months and years. You need to match your observation window to the business's tempo—not the market's.

For most long-term investors, this means committing to an initial 6- or 12-month no-action window unless there's a material deterioration in fundamentals. During this period, you do not adjust your position based on price alone. You monitor earnings reports, industry developments, and changes in leadership, but you don't make impulsive exits. You observe. You collect. You think. And each check-in is documented in your journal—brief summaries of what's happening, what you're feeling, and whether your thesis still holds. This creates a slow, deliberate rhythm that reinforces composure over chaos.

What distinguishes the best investors is not their ability to predict price movements, but their skill in interpreting unfolding reality with patience. Consider the example of investors who held Amazon in the early 2000s. The stock fell over 90% during the dot-com crash. Yet for those who understood its infrastructure ambitions, customer obsession, and long-term scalability, the temporary collapse in price did not invalidate the investment case. Those who exited out of fear missed one of the greatest compounding stories in modern market history. Those who anchored themselves in understanding—not sentiment—prospered.

There's a deeper lesson here: your emotional stability is correlated to the clarity of your convictions. And clarity is earned, not inherited. It comes from doing the mental labour of truly understanding what you own and why. That is why the act of ownership must be accompanied by reflective practice. Without it, you become a reactive participant in markets—chasing comfort and avoiding discomfort. But with it, you begin to think like an owner. And owners endure.

This shift also allows you to confront a hard truth: *even good decisions can produce bad outcomes in the short term*. The market is not a morality play. It does not reward virtue in predictable timeframes. You can make a rational investment based on sound analysis and still experience short-term drawdowns. That is not failure. That is friction. And if you expect investing to be a frictionless path to wealth, you will abandon good strategies at the first sign of pain. The journal reminds you: outcomes must be interpreted in light of intentions and process. If your process was sound and your logic intact, the outcome—however uncomfortable—is part of the broader statistical canvas of long-term investing.

A second benefit of consistent post-purchase reflection is that it builds a database of personal decision-making. Over time, patterns emerge. You begin to notice when you're prone to overconfidence, or when you ignore red flags because you're emotionally invested in a brand. You learn which industries you tend to understand well, and which you romanticise without sufficient depth. This is your edge—not in beating others, but in better knowing yourself. The market is a mirror. The clearer you can see your own habits and heuristics, the less likely you are to sabotage your own returns.

The Stock Memory Journal also teaches you that silence is a decision. Not acting is not the same as being passive. It is often a deliberate choice to wait, observe, and protect your process from unnecessary disturbance. This insight is critical in a media environment that incentivises perpetual reaction. Every financial headline screams urgency. Every influencer has a hot take. Every chart promises insight. But wisdom in investing often looks like boredom. It looks like waiting, watching, and doing nothing—because your work was done when you chose the stock, and your job now is to let the business work.

To support this process, some investors schedule fixed review intervals—quarterly or biannually—where they conduct a structured reflection. This includes reviewing recent company developments, comparing them to original expectations, and evaluating whether the thesis has strengthened, weakened, or remained intact. These reviews are not emotional check-ins. They are analytical audits. They separate the question "Has the stock dropped?" from "Has the business deteriorated?" One is noise; the other is signal.

Ultimately, the day after you own a stock is when your character begins to matter more than your information. Every investor starts with roughly the same data: financial statements, market news, and analyst reports. But what you do with that data—how you integrate it, weigh it, respond to it—depends on the emotional infrastructure you've built. The Stock Memory Journal is how you lay that foundation. It's how you convert knowledge into judgement, and judgement into discipline.

Owning something doesn't just change your portfolio; it changes how you think. You become attuned to macro developments not out of curiosity but because you're exposed. You follow regulatory trends, earnings surprises, competitive threats—not as distant events, but as variables that affect your assets. You start to think like a businessperson, not a bystander. This is the psychological transformation that investing promises—but only if you embrace the reflective, deliberate practice of ownership.

The act of buying a stock is easy. The act of owning it well is not. It requires structure, memory, observation, and the humility to admit when your thesis breaks. But it also gives you something rare: the ability to operate in a noisy world with internal calm. That is what the Stock Memory Journal cultivates—a space for insight, a record of thinking, and a guide for navigating the emotional terrain that begins the moment you press *buy*.

Chapter 4
Dividends, Growth, and the Stories Behind Returns:

We do not invest in companies in abstraction; we invest in what we anticipate they will deliver—and that delivery is far from uniform. Returns manifest in different forms, carrying varied names and shaped by distinct philosophies and expectations. One investor may seek a steady, almost meditative stream of quarterly income, compounding quietly in the background, offering the reassurance of consistency. Another may chase the dramatic potential of capital growth, staking on a company whose present earnings are modest but whose future might dominate markets, justifying risk. As one delves deeper, it becomes clear: returns are never merely financial—they are reflections of belief, temperament, and life stage. Grasping them begins with looking beyond the numbers.

This chapter does not chase returns; it seeks to decode them. It examines the distinction between income and growth not just as financial mechanics but as narratives that shape portfolio architecture. Consider the dividend. It is more than a payment—it is a signal. A dividend communicates maturity, cash flow discipline, and sometimes limitation. A company that distributes dividends has often passed its aggressive reinvestment phase, producing more cash than it can immediately redeploy. Generosity may disguise shortsightedness; conservatism can conceal prudence. The investor's challenge lies in interpreting this language without overlaying assumptions.

Growth investing, by contrast, appeals to those drawn to possibility. The argument: the future is insufficiently priced today. A company expanding rapidly—gaining customers, margins, and scale—may command a premium valuation. Yet such investing demands belief in the sustainability of that trajectory. It requires scrutiny: moats, execution risk, scalability, conversion of growth into profit. And psychologically, it tests patience: volatility, long horizons, and the temptation to equate rising prices with underlying strength. Popularity is seductive; substance requires discernment.

Early in one's investing journey, the most crucial decision may not be which stock to select, but what kind of return to prioritise. This is a spectrum, not a binary choice, and it colours evaluation criteria, holding periods, success metrics, and susceptibility to market noise. Are you at a life stage where recurring income comforts you? Or do you favour backing businesses before the wider market recognises their full potential? Neither path is inherently superior; each carries distinct emotional and financial consequences.

Context shapes strategy. A retiree dependent on investment income faces different imperatives than a thirty-year-old with decades of compounding ahead. Yet age is only part of the equation; psychology is equally decisive. Some investors sleep easier knowing their assets generate tangible income, others tolerate fluctuation for potential upside. Alignment is paramount: philosophy must suit both practical needs and psychological bandwidth.

Dividends, however, are not uniform. A six per cent yield may appear attractive yet mask declining revenues, rising leverage, or unsustainable payouts. High yields often signal distress. Dividend investors must dig beneath the surface: is the payout supported by earnings? Is the ratio sustainable? Has the company historically maintained or grown distributions across cycles? These are not abstract queries—they are questions of reliability.

Growth stocks pose distinct challenges. They often pay no income, and valuation rests on projected potential rather than present performance. The peril is narrative, not merely finance. Compelling stories are common; credible ones less so. Investors must distinguish genuine momentum from hype. Is growth building defensible advantage? Does revenue convert to free cash flow? Are customers loyal, or merely incentivised temporarily? Nuance is critical; when the story falters, so does the price.

Mature portfolios rarely consist solely of one type. Resilient strategies often blend dividend and growth, shifting over time. Younger investors may favour growth-heavy allocations, later rebalancing towards dividends to secure stability, predictability, and income. Intentionality remains essential: every holding should serve a purpose, its role articulated—not merely in expected returns, but in function: compounding capital, generating income, or mitigating volatility.

Understanding returns also entails recognising personal biases. Investors overestimate tolerance for volatility in calm markets, undervalue income until necessity arises. Some pursue dividends without probing underlying risks, mistaking regularity for strength. The antidote is reflection: what function should investments serve? Which trade-offs are acceptable? What investing narrative is intellectually and emotionally sustainable? These are identity questions, not technical ones.

This chapter equips you to answer them. You will learn to evaluate dividends contextually, approach growth with rigour and curiosity, and craft a philosophy attuned to your goals, temperament, horizon, and tolerance for uncertainty. Returns are not generic; they are by-products of decisions made under uncertainty, informed by insight, and bounded by reality. Understanding them—where they originate, what sustains them, and how they align with your needs—transforms investing from chasing outcomes to cultivating them. That is the essence of intelligent investing. And it begins here.

Income vs Expansion: Two Philosophies of Reward:

Every investor is, consciously or not, making a philosophical choice about how they wish to be rewarded. Do you want your investments to pay you regularly in the form of dividends—concrete, bankable income that shows up with reassuring consistency? Or do you want your investments to grow in value over time, with the promise of significant capital appreciation down the line? These aren't just technical differences. They reflect deeper questions about your temperament, financial needs, emotional bandwidth, and beliefs about what risk really means.

The debate between dividend income and growth investing is often presented as a binary, but that framing is overly simplistic. Both approaches represent different ways of engaging with the idea of ownership. A dividend-paying company says: *We have matured to the point where we no longer need to reinvest all of our earnings. So we return a portion to you.* A growth-focused company says: *We believe every penny of retained earnings is better spent fuelling expansion.* Neither message is inherently better. But each implies a different vision for the future—and a different role for you as an investor.

Dividends offer psychological clarity. You buy a stock. It pays you cash. You can spend it, reinvest it, or save it. The value exchange is immediate and tangible. For many investors—especially those in or approaching retirement—this regular stream of income serves both as financial support and emotional assurance. It mitigates the pressure to sell shares during market downturns, since some return is flowing in regardless of price movement. This is particularly valuable when markets are volatile and confidence is low. You don't have to *believe* in a speculative future—you're already being paid today.

Yet dividends are not without nuance. A company may pay a high yield because its stock price has declined, not because its business is strong. An unsustainably high payout ratio—the percentage of earnings paid out as dividends—can signal a business straining to maintain investor confidence rather than reinvesting wisely. If dividends are being funded by debt, or if they leave the company without enough retained earnings for innovation or expansion, the short-term gratification comes at long-term cost. Evaluating dividend stocks, then, requires more than yield-chasing. It requires assessing the underlying cash flow health, capital allocation priorities, and resilience across business cycles.

Growth investing presents a different relationship with time. You're not being paid today. You're being asked to wait. Your reward, if it comes, will be in the form of rising share prices driven by expanding revenues, increasing margins, and strategic execution. You are, in effect, co-signing a belief that the business will become more valuable in the future than it is today. This requires a longer holding horizon, greater patience, and a more nuanced understanding of business dynamics. Growth investors often tolerate higher volatility because they are anchoring their confidence in the company's trajectory, not its quarterly payouts.

The allure of growth investing is particularly strong in environments where capital is abundant and interest rates are low. In such periods, investors gravitate towards innovation, disruption, and scale. But growth investing also carries the risk of narrative-driven exuberance. When future promises are priced too generously into today's valuations, even strong execution can disappoint. The classic example is the dot-com era, where companies with no profits—and in many cases, no revenues—commanded enormous market capitalisations. The lesson is not to avoid growth stocks, but to interrogate the foundations of the growth story. What is the source of competitive advantage? Is there a path to profitability? Are customer acquisition costs decreasing over time? Real growth investing is not about chasing high price-to-earnings multiples; it's about identifying businesses with enduring economics, scalable models, and disciplined capital use.

Your personal orientation toward income or growth often reflects more than your stage of life. It reflects your psychological makeup. Some investors take comfort in predictability. Others thrive on potential. Income-focused investors often prefer to *harvest* returns, building portfolios that create a sense of ongoing reward. Growth-focused investors are more willing to *plant and wait*, tolerating periods of underperformance in exchange for longer-term upside. There's no moral high ground here. The question is: which approach better supports your financial goals and emotional discipline?

Consider two investors: one is a mid-career professional with a stable income, a long runway to retirement, and a relatively high tolerance for market swings. This person may benefit from a growth-oriented portfolio, where returns are reinvested and compounded over decades. Their primary constraint is time, not cash flow. The second investor is recently retired, with a finite nest egg and no interest in speculating. For them, the priority is income generation and capital preservation. A portfolio of high-quality dividend-paying stocks—perhaps supplemented with bonds or REITs—may provide both the stability and liquidity required to fund living expenses without regular asset sales. Neither strategy is objectively better. They are fit-for-purpose responses to different personal circumstances.

But even this dichotomy is increasingly outdated. Many modern portfolios blend the two approaches, recognising that the best companies often exhibit characteristics of both. Some firms generate strong free cash flow, maintain moderate dividend payouts, and still reinvest effectively for growth. Others offer modest yields that grow consistently year over year, blending the psychological comfort of income with the strategic upside of long-term expansion. Think of companies like Johnson & Johnson, Microsoft, or Unilever. These are not startups chasing hypergrowth, but neither are they static income machines. They are businesses with track records of capital discipline, shareholder respect, and strategic reinvestment.

The real value lies in clarity—understanding what you're buying, why you're buying it, and how it fits into your overall strategy. Investing blindly into high-yield stocks without understanding the business model or capital structure is no less dangerous than throwing money at unprofitable tech companies based on headlines. Your portfolio is a reflection of your judgement. That includes not only what you believe about the market, but also what you believe about your own behaviour. Can you stomach seeing your portfolio drop 30% if you know the underlying businesses are still solid? Can you resist the temptation to sell a stock just because it stopped paying a dividend for a quarter? These are not abstract hypotheticals. They are emotional tests you will face.

One of the most helpful practices for any investor is to periodically assess not just performance, but *philosophical alignment.* Are your investments serving your needs? Have your needs changed? Do you feel confident in your holdings—or are you holding them because you feel stuck, overwhelmed, or unsure of what else to do? Your preference for income or growth will evolve. The best portfolios are not frozen in time. They are living structures that respond to shifting goals, markets, and life circumstances.

As you read the next sections of this chapter, treat dividend yield and capital appreciation not as competing ideologies, but as tools. Learn how to evaluate each on its own merits. Understand the tax implications, the behavioural triggers, the business signals behind each return stream. Ask yourself what kind of reward feels most aligned with your temperament—not just what sounds good in theory. Because when your investment philosophy matches your psychology, something important happens: you stop reacting, and start deciding.

Clarity is not just a strategy. It's a form of psychological protection. And in investing, that protection is often worth more than the returns themselves.

What a Dividend Tells You (and What It Doesn't):

A dividend looks simple. You own a share. The company pays you money. That's it. But this simplicity is deceptive. Behind every dividend lies a cascade of strategic decisions, operational performance, and capital allocation philosophy. And for the investor, understanding what a dividend does—and *does not*—communicate is essential. A dividend can signal strength, maturity, and commitment. It can also mask stagnation, poor reinvestment opportunities, or even financial strain. Interpreting dividends correctly is not about yield-chasing. It's about learning to read a company's character through how it treats its capital.

Start with this principle: *A dividend is not a gift. It is a policy decision.* When a business distributes part of its earnings to shareholders, it is making a trade-off. That money could have been reinvested to fund growth, reduce debt, acquire another business, or strengthen the balance sheet. By paying it out, management is effectively saying: *We believe shareholders are better served receiving this cash now than waiting for us to deploy it internally.* This is a significant claim. It implies a level of maturity in the business, a degree of cash flow consistency, and a sober view of where future value can realistically come from.

But not all dividends deserve applause. A high dividend yield—often mistaken for generosity—can be misleading. Yield is a function of two variables: the dividend per share and the stock price. When share prices fall sharply and the dividend remains unchanged, the yield rises. This can create the illusion of value where there is, in fact, distress. A utility company with a 4% yield backed by stable cash flows is fundamentally different from a declining retailer whose 10% yield exists only because investors are fleeing. The market is not always right—but it is often directionally informative. A very high yield should trigger scrutiny, not excitement.

Evaluating dividend sustainability requires examining the *payout ratio*—the percentage of earnings paid out as dividends. A company that pays out 30–50% of its earnings often strikes a prudent balance, retaining enough for reinvestment while rewarding shareholders. But ratios exceeding 70%—and especially those above 100%—suggest fragility. Either earnings are under pressure, or management is propping up the dividend to maintain appearances. Neither scenario bodes well. A cut may be imminent, and with it, a likely decline in share price. This is where dividend investing can go wrong: when investors conflate historical yield with future security.

Consider the case of General Electric. Once a dividend aristocrat, it maintained payouts even as its fundamentals deteriorated. The dividend became symbolic—a promise to shareholders that stability endured. But when the business reality caught up, the dividend was slashed, and the stock tumbled. Contrast this with Apple, which for years paid no dividend at all, despite massive profitability. Its reinvestment opportunities were strong, its capital discipline unmatched, and shareholders were rewarded through appreciation. Only after its growth engine matured did it begin returning capital. The point isn't to glorify or demonise either model—but to understand that dividends reflect strategic philosophy more than investor benevolence.

Another subtlety: dividends are sticky. Companies are slow to raise them when earnings improve, and even slower to cut them when conditions worsen. This is partly psychological—investors punish dividend cuts severely—and partly structural. Many institutional investors hold dividend-paying stocks precisely for the income stream. A cut can force redemptions or violate mandate constraints. As a result, management teams tend to protect dividends, even at the expense of optimal capital deployment. They may borrow to sustain payouts. They may delay necessary investment. This rigidity creates risks that aren't always visible in a yield figure.

Yet dividends also send credible signals. When a company raises its dividend regularly—especially through economic cycles—it communicates confidence in its cash generation, operational discipline, and shareholder alignment. This is why "dividend growth investing" focuses less on current yield and more on consistency of increases. A firm that grows its dividend 6–8% annually for a decade is telling you something powerful: *We are profitable, we are stable, and we respect your role in our success.* These are not marketing slogans. They are evidenced in policy.

Understanding what a dividend doesn't tell you is just as vital. A dividend does not guarantee stability. It does not guarantee performance. It does not mean management is wise. It does not protect you from poor strategic decisions, declining industries, or structural disruption. Owning a dividend stock is not the same as owning a bond. The payout is discretionary, and subject to change. And when it changes, it often happens abruptly—without warning, during moments of broader financial stress, when you are least prepared.

There is also a behavioural risk. Dividends can lull investors into complacency. Receiving income regularly can create the illusion that all is well, even if the share price is deteriorating or the industry is undergoing secular decline. This "income trap" can lead investors to ignore warning signs. The focus on yield becomes a crutch. The investor stops analysing the business. They become an income collector rather than an owner. This is not investing. It is a passive dependency.

Conversely, some of the most disciplined capital allocators eschew dividends altogether. Berkshire Hathaway famously reinvests every dollar of retained earnings. Why? Because Warren Buffett believes he can generate superior returns within the business. Shareholders trust that philosophy because he has a track record of doing so. The absence of a dividend, in this case, is not a sign of indifference—it's a bet on compounding. This underlines a critical point: the best dividend policy is the one that aligns with the company's strategic opportunity set, not the investor's short-term preference.

As an investor, your task is not to seek yield in isolation, but to understand *what underpins it.* Is the company's free cash flow sufficient to support the dividend without sacrificing growth? Is debt rising while distributions are maintained? Are there better uses of capital that are being ignored? Do management's incentives align with sustainable shareholder returns, or are they placating a restless base with temporary payouts? These are the questions that elevate dividend investing from simplistic screening to informed ownership.

Taxes add another layer of complexity. In some jurisdictions, dividend income is taxed less favourably than capital gains. This makes high-yield strategies less attractive for certain investors, particularly those in higher income brackets. In others, tax-advantaged accounts may allow dividends to accumulate without immediate penalty. Understanding these implications is not just a matter of compliance. It is a matter of net return—the only kind that matters in the end.

Dividends can be powerful. They can compound when reinvested. They can provide psychological ballast during downturns. They can fund lifestyles, charities, and future investments. But they are not immune to context. In evaluating a dividend, always ask: *Is this a return of excess capital, or a distraction from a lack of ideas? Is this sustainable income, or borrowed confidence?* Learning to make that distinction is not a technical skill—it is a mindset.

A wise investor does not simply collect dividends. They interpret them. They decode the signal, question the motive, assess the trade-offs. Because when you look beneath the yield, you often find the real story. And in investing, as in life, it's the story that matters.

Growth Investing and the Myth of the Future-Proof Company:

The seduction of growth is timeless. It is the story of tomorrow told in numbers—of untapped markets, rising revenue curves, and imagined dominance. Few things excite the human imagination like acceleration. And in the world of investing, growth companies offer a potent promise: that what they are today is only a pale reflection of what they will become. But this narrative, compelling as it is, often obscures a harder truth: *not all fast-growing companies are built to last.* And the most dangerous assumption a new investor can make is to mistake velocity for durability.

Growth investing thrives on optimism, and rightly so. The best-performing stocks of the past half-century—Amazon, Apple, Alphabet, Nvidia—were once volatile growth stories that defied scepticism and delivered exponential returns. But these companies are exceptions, not archetypes. For every enduring growth titan, there are dozens of others whose trajectory followed a predictable arc: a dramatic rise, euphoric valuation, managerial overreach, and eventual decline or irrelevance. The investor's job is not merely to spot growth, but to *distinguish between growth that compounds and growth that burns out.*

What fuels hype is often visibility, not viability. A consumer app that adds 10 million users in a quarter makes headlines. A SaaS platform that triples revenue in two years commands sky-high multiples. But growth without economic resilience is a sugar rush. The key question is not how fast a company is growing, but *how well that growth is being earned and what it costs to sustain it.* A business losing money on every sale, hoping to "make it up on volume", is not innovating—it's gambling.

To filter hype from substance, start with unit economics. If a company can't make a profit at the level of a single customer or transaction, no amount of scale will rescue it. Uber, for years, embodied this dilemma. Its growth was stunning, but deeply subsidised. It was only much later that the economics began to stabilise, and even then, not uniformly across markets. Similarly, WeWork's explosive expansion masked a broken business model. Occupancy and branding disguised cash burn and misaligned incentives. Growth, in both cases, served as camouflage for fragility.

Next, examine the *source* of the company's growth. Is it organic—driven by genuine demand—or is it acquisition-fuelled? Are customers returning, or is churn quietly eroding gains? Is the pricing power evident, or is discounting required to stay relevant? *Sustainable growth stems from customer loyalty, not customer bribery.* If revenue grows but gross margins compress, something fundamental is being eroded. The company may be building revenue but destroying value.

Market size, too, is often misunderstood. A large total addressable market (TAM) means nothing if the company lacks a defensible edge. Many investors get seduced by scale: "if we can just capture 2% of a $100 billion market…" But *markets do not distribute revenue evenly.* They reward competitive advantage, brand strength, and operational discipline. A future-proof company is not one with a large playground—it's one with a castle and a moat.

This brings us to competitive durability. What protects the company from being copied, outspent, or leapfrogged? Is there a network effect, a proprietary asset, a switching cost? Or is the business essentially replicable, its margins a temporary artifact of being first to market? True future-proofing comes not from being early, but from being entrenched. Netflix's transition from DVD rental to global streaming was not just a pivot—it was a masterclass in reinvestment, risk-taking, and cultural foresight. Others followed, but Netflix's infrastructure, data advantage, and brand capital allowed it to endure the onslaught.

One of the most important filters for evaluating growth companies is leadership integrity and capital discipline. *How management behaves when flush with capital tells you more than any earnings report.* Do they reinvest prudently or acquire recklessly? Do they dilute shareholders through excessive stock-based compensation? Are they transparent about trade-offs, or do they overpromise in quarterly calls and investor decks? When vision outpaces execution, growth becomes a liability.

Valuation is where many growth investors abandon rigour. The common defence is that great companies are "always expensive"—and there's some truth to that. But price matters. Not because cheap is good, but because expectations are embedded in valuation. A company trading at 40 times earnings must justify it not once, but *every quarter*. The higher the multiple, the narrower the margin for error. Tesla's stock, for instance, soared on the back of revolutionary ambition—but that same ambition now requires consistent delivery. Investors who entered late in the hype cycle discovered that even visionary businesses can disappoint when the narrative overtakes the numbers.

Growth investing, at its best, is not speculative. It is disciplined optimism. It involves asking: *what would have to remain true for this company to thrive a decade from now?* Are those assumptions economic, cultural, or technological? Are they within management's control, or do they hinge on unpredictable variables like regulation or consumer behaviour? Zoom, for example, exploded during the pandemic, but sustaining that momentum in a hybridising world requires more than name recognition. It requires evolution.

A useful mental model for evaluating growth is the "S-curve". Companies often begin with slow adoption, followed by explosive growth, then a plateau. The plateau is where many businesses stumble—they either stagnate or reinvent. Amazon, famously, reinvested through every phase, launching AWS, expanding logistics, and entering new verticals. Others, like Blackberry, dominated briefly but failed to adapt. Recognising *where a company is on its S-curve* helps frame whether current growth is the beginning, the middle, or the end.

Investors should also resist the cult of the founder. Charisma is not strategy. Vision is not execution. Many growth companies are led by charismatic figures who command media cycles and investor loyalty. But unless the company has institutionalised its advantage—through systems, governance, and reinvestment strategy—it remains fragile. Theranos is a cautionary tale, but even more mainstream examples show this risk. Elon Musk may be brilliant, but his presence introduces volatility as much as value. A durable company should outlive the personality at the helm.

Finally, remember that *future-proof is not a category—it is a process.* It is built year by year, through consistent execution, strategic adaptability, and respect for capital. Growth investing becomes dangerous when it is reduced to storytelling. A compelling narrative is not the same as durable economics. Your job as an investor is not to predict the next Apple. It is to understand why Apple succeeded—then assess whether those same patterns are visible elsewhere.

Filters for separating substance from hype are not formulas. They are frameworks. Look for understandable business models. Study cash flow, not just revenue. Assess competitive advantage, not just market size. Track insider behaviour, not just media buzz. Focus on return on invested capital, not just user growth. And above all, ask: *if this company stopped growing tomorrow, would it still be worth owning?* If the answer is no, what you're holding is not an investment—it's a bet.

The myth of the future-proof company persists because it flatters our desire for certainty in an uncertain world. But certainty is not the foundation of good investing—clarity is. And clarity begins when we stop chasing growth for its own sake and start asking what it's really made of.

Building a Blended Philosophy That Matches Your Life Stage:

Every investor must answer, eventually, a deceptively simple question: *what do you want your money to do for you—and when?* It is not enough to chase returns in the abstract. Investment must serve your real-world needs, which evolve with time. The beauty and challenge of long-term investing is that you are not just building a portfolio—you are designing a life-support system. That system, if it is to endure and perform, must be deliberately aligned with your goals, your temperament, and—critically—your stage of life.

Dividend investing and growth investing are often positioned as rival camps: income versus appreciation, stability versus ambition, the present versus the future. In truth, this is a false dichotomy. Most serious investors do not pick sides between dividends and growth. Instead, they *blend*, constructing a philosophy that adapts to their financial context. This blend is not static. It should adjust over time, much like how a person adjusts their nutritional intake based on age, energy levels, and activity demands. A young professional in their thirties has different needs and tolerances than a retiree in their seventies. Yet both can build powerful portfolios—if they anchor their choices in clarity rather than ideology.

Dividends provide tangible, periodic cash flows. That cash can be reinvested to accelerate compounding or withdrawn to fund living expenses. Dividend-paying companies often exhibit mature business models, conservative capital allocation, and greater predictability in earnings. This stability can serve as a psychological anchor—especially during periods of market volatility. Knowing that your holdings are *paying you to wait* introduces a discipline that pure growth investing often lacks.

Growth stocks, by contrast, typically reinvest their profits to fund expansion—new markets, new products, R&D, or acquisitions. These businesses may deliver no cash flow to shareholders in the short term, but their internal compounding can result in significant capital appreciation if the execution is sound. The price of this upside is patience and volatility. And not all investors are built for it. *Growth investing rewards vision but punishes impatience.* Those who sell at the first dip miss the full arc of value creation.

The question, then, is not "which is better?" but "which balance suits you now?" This is where life stage becomes an indispensable guide. If you are early in your wealth-building years, your most precious asset is time. Volatility is not a threat; it's a feature—an invitation to buy quality businesses at temporary discounts. At this stage, a tilt toward growth makes sense, provided the underlying companies are financially sound and competitively advantaged. Dividends may still have a place—particularly if they are reinvested—but their immediate cash value is secondary.

As you approach midlife, the priorities often shift. Your earnings may peak, your financial responsibilities expand, and your risk tolerance may narrow. Here, many investors begin to introduce a *balance*—a barbell portfolio with a blend of compounders on one end and income-generating assets on the other. You're no longer betting on an either-or proposition; you're orchestrating multiple instruments to play in harmony. Growth ensures long-term capital preservation and upside. Dividends provide intermediate liquidity and reduce the need to sell during drawdowns.

In retirement or pre-retirement, the calculus shifts again. Liquidity and consistency become paramount. Investors at this stage often lean toward high-quality dividend payers—not for their yield alone, but for their *reliability*. A business with a strong balance sheet, modest payout ratio, and decades-long dividend track record is more than a source of income—it's a financial ally. That said, even retirees can benefit from retaining some exposure to growth. Longevity risk—the possibility of outliving your savings—is real, and inflation continues its quiet erosion. A portion of the portfolio must be positioned to grow meaningfully over the next decade or two.

This adaptive blending is not just a technical choice—it is a philosophical stance. It recognises that investing is not static and that wisdom lies in flexibility, not rigidity. You may begin your investing life enamoured with the excitement of growth stories, only to later discover the peace of dividend reliability. Or you may build a steady base of income holdings, then gradually layer in secular growth winners as your confidence grows. *There is no shame in evolving—only in remaining dogmatic in the face of changing needs.*

Practical implementation requires more than preference. It demands method. Start by identifying your goals—not abstract ones like "I want to retire rich", but specific ones: "I want £2,000 per month in passive income by age 60" or "I want my portfolio to double in value within the next 15 years without relying on leverage". These goals determine your time horizon, income needs, and risk capacity. From there, reverse-engineer your asset mix. A goal rooted in passive income lends itself to dividend aristocrats, REITs, and utility stocks. A goal centred on long-term wealth creation may prioritise category-leading innovators in technology, healthcare, or global consumer brands.

The key, however, is not merely asset selection—it is *role assignment.* Every holding in your portfolio should have a defined purpose. Is it there to generate income? To provide downside protection? To deliver asymmetric growth? To hedge inflation? When assets lose their role—or fail to fulfil it—they must be re-evaluated or removed. This functional clarity is what separates thoughtful investing from random accumulation.

Consider, for example, an investor in their early 40s, earning a strong salary and with no imminent need for portfolio income. They might allocate 70% of their capital to long-term growth companies with reinvested earnings and high ROIC, and 30% to dividend payers offering modest but growing yields. This dividend allocation may act as a psychological ballast and a source of optional liquidity—should career disruptions or opportunities arise. Fast forward twenty years, and that same investor may flip the ratio: 70% of capital flowing from reliable income sources to fund life, with a growth sleeve providing longevity and optionality.

What's critical is not the precise ratio, but the thought process. *Your investment mix should reflect your actual life—not an abstract risk tolerance score.* If your job is precarious, income from stable assets matters more. If your expenses are covered by a pension, growth can be emphasised without fear. If you're supporting family, liquidity matters. If you're unencumbered and well-capitalised, patience and volatility may be welcome allies.

Another factor that shapes this balance is temperament. Some investors simply sleep better knowing they are receiving dividends. Others are energised by disruptive trends and asymmetric bets. Neither mindset is inherently superior—but both require discipline. Income investors must guard against yield-chasing, which often leads to unstable or over-leveraged companies. Growth investors must resist the lure of storytelling over substance. A blended philosophy acknowledges these biases and creates a framework for counterbalancing them.

Critically, blending growth and dividends does not mean watering down your convictions. It means structuring them in a way that aligns with your evolving needs. You are not building a monument to ideology—you are designing a toolkit for real life. Just as a well-trained athlete cross-trains to build endurance, flexibility, and strength, an investor blends strategies to enhance resilience, adaptability, and performance.

The final piece of this puzzle is review. A blended philosophy is not a set-and-forget exercise. Life changes—sometimes subtly, sometimes abruptly. Careers shift, families grow, health fluctuates, markets turn. Your portfolio must be reviewed periodically through the lens of your updated life stage and objectives. What once made sense may now be misaligned. Course correction is not failure—it's wisdom.

Ultimately, blending dividend and growth investing is not a compromise—it is an expression of maturity. It reflects a mindset that values both security and aspiration, both present needs and future ambitions. It recognises that financial life is not linear and that the best investors are those who *think in decades but act in quarters*—adjusting steadily while staying anchored in purpose.

A portfolio is not just a collection of stocks. It is a reflection of how you interpret the trade-offs between now and later, between certainty and potential, between what you need and what you hope for. The art of blending is the art of reconciling those trade-offs into a strategy you can trust—*not just when markets rise, but when life gets complicated.*

Chapter 5
Long-Term Vision, Short-Term Nerves:

The modern investor exists in a perpetual tension. Long-term wealth creation demands patience, detachment, and sustained conviction, yet every day delivers an unceasing torrent of data, alerts, and narratives engineered to provoke reaction. Markets open with fresh prices and frayed nerves. Analysts issue forecasts. News cycles reward volatility over context. And in the midst of this, the individual investor is expected to maintain a decade-spanning perspective. It is no small ask—and psychologically, few are fully equipped.

This chapter begins with a candid admission: the hardest part of investing is not identifying opportunities—it is holding steady in conviction. Especially when screens flash numbers that contradict your thesis, or when others panic, euphoria spreads, or the crowd moves faster than you. Patience is not passivity; it is a sustained exercise in self-control. It is the most potent advantage a long-term investor can cultivate.

Across generations, the most reliable market performers share a deceptively simple trait: they remained invested. Their edge was not clairvoyance, but constancy. Time in the market—through recessions, corrections, and recoveries—proved more powerful than timing it. Consider Ronald Read, a janitor in Vermont, who passed away in 2014 leaving an estate exceeding $8 million. He neither founded companies nor managed hedge funds; he bought shares of stable, dividend-paying businesses and held them for decades. No leverage, no algorithms, just patience and consistency. Meanwhile, some brilliant analysts fail to outperform not for lack of intellect, but for lack of restraint.

This chapter addresses how to navigate markets with clarity while resisting the temptation to react to every fluctuation. Volatility is mathematically inevitable, yet psychologically misinterpreted. A 20% drawdown is normal, yet many perceive it as catastrophe, confusing short-term movement with fundamental decay, and sabotaging their own strategies in the process.

The remedy is neither ignorance nor numbness. It lies in cultivating systems of understanding and discipline—frameworks that differentiate genuine risk from noise. When a holding drops 15% in a week, the critical question is not "What is the price doing?" but "Has the business fundamentally changed?" Is the model impaired? Have customer behaviours shifted? Has leverage risen to unsustainable levels? If the answer is no, the price movement reflects sentiment, not substance.

Humans are wired to react to threat. A declining chart triggers the same neural pathways as physical danger. In investing, this instinct can be a liability. The best investors reinterpret discomfort as a cue for curiosity, not action. Rituals, routines, and mental frameworks provide insulation against reactive impulses.

This chapter outlines strategies for constructing such frameworks. Emotions are not suppressed—they are structured. Daily, weekly, and quarterly check-ins focus attention on what truly matters. Journaling—recording decisions, hypotheses, and reflections—builds a historical record of how beliefs respond under pressure, creating a body of evidence for more measured responses in future.

Historical exemplars reinforce this approach. Benjamin Graham's "Mr Market" metaphor remains instructive: the market is an erratic partner offering prices at whim. You are free to transact or decline, but never compelled to internalise its mood as truth. Volatility becomes opportunity, not threat. Similarly, excessive information exposure erodes clarity. Frequent monitoring magnifies normal variance into illusory signal. This chapter advocates evaluating holdings with the detachment of a CEO: at fixed intervals, against meaningful metrics, with a focus on trajectory rather than chatter.

Underlying all guidance is a mindset shift: investing is a test of stamina, not speed. Success emerges from consistent allocation, not rapid response. Action is overrated; restraint, undervalued. If a business remains fundamentally sound, the optimal choice is often to hold. Yet holding can feel like inaction, provoking cognitive dissonance and the temptation to sell simply to regain a sense of control.

Understanding one's psychological architecture is crucial. Are you anxious when portfolios fall, or when peers advance faster? Do you seek information for clarity or comfort? Do you evaluate companies or narratives? Your answers inform the rituals and boundaries that sustain long-term investing practice. No universal protocol exists; what matters is alignment with your cognitive and emotional reality.

Practically, this chapter is about cultivating resilient investor behaviour. Market stress is a design problem, not a test of willpower. Athletes rehearse composure under pressure; investors can do the same. Not every day requires decision-making, but every day shapes temperament.

Drawdowns, crashes, rallies, and bubbles are inevitable. Professionals distinguish themselves not by avoiding these events, but by interpreting them accurately. A 25% paper loss is a test of thesis, not a signal of doom. Fear is contextualised, not eliminated. Markets are noisy, capricious, and opinionated. Your role is to remain anchored—to process, values, and reality. Wealth accumulates not by reacting to volatility, but by compounding through it.

You are not a speculator chasing immediate gratification. You are a steward of capital, constructing an enterprise intended to endure. The tension between long-term vision and short-term nerves is real, yet navigable. With deliberate habits, structured frameworks, and disciplined mindset, your investing self can thrive amidst motion—not by denying emotion, but by leveraging time, the one advantage immune to replication, hacking, or arbitrage.

Why Time Is the Only True Edge:

The most powerful edge in investing is not hidden in algorithms, insider access, predictive analytics, or financial sophistication. It lies in something far less glamorous: the ability to wait. Not just for weeks or quarters, but for years—sometimes decades—without losing conviction, composure, or alignment with your core principles. In a marketplace that rewards immediacy and punishes hesitation, *time is not a passive force—it is the ultimate competitive advantage.*

This insight is neither new nor theoretical. It is supported by a century's worth of market data and the biographies of virtually every investor who achieved enduring success. From Warren Buffett to John Templeton, from Charlie Munger to Shelby Davis, the pattern is strikingly consistent: wealth did not arrive all at once, but rather through the slow, steady compounding of capital held in high-quality businesses. Their edge was not prediction, but duration. And in a landscape dominated by speed, duration is the least replicable strategy of all.

But what does it mean, concretely, to invest with time as your edge? It means resisting the dopamine rush of short-term wins in favour of long-term alignment. It means understanding that *the true driver of investment returns is not stock selection, but the uninterrupted power of compounding*. Consider a stock that grows earnings at 10% per year. In a one-year window, that gain is marginal. Over a decade, it doubles. Over thirty years, it multiplies more than seventeen-fold. But only if you let it.

The problem is psychological, not mathematical. Time is intellectually obvious and emotionally difficult. Patience feels like inaction. In an age of endless stimulation, doing nothing can feel like negligence. Yet that stillness—anchored by discipline rather than inertia—is precisely where most of your long-term outperformance will come from. *The market offers opportunities to anyone. But it only rewards those who can delay gratification with precision and resolve.*

Ronald Read understood this. A gas station attendant and janitor from Vermont, Read died with an estate worth over $8 million. His secret? He lived modestly and invested consistently in blue-chip, dividend-paying companies, holding them for decades. No hedge funds. No high-frequency trades. No newsletter subscriptions. His portfolio reflected what most investors claim to believe, but few are willing to practise: that staying power beats cleverness. Read didn't need to be brilliant. He needed to be patient.

Contrast this with the average retail investor, who typically underperforms the very funds they invest in—*not because the funds are poorly managed, but because the investors abandon them prematurely.* Data from Dalbar and Morningstar routinely show that the average investor captures only a fraction of the returns their funds generate, simply because they buy high and sell low. They chase performance. They flinch at volatility. They act when they should wait. The problem is not the market. It is our relationship with time.

That relationship is fragile because it's tested daily. Every tick in the market, every headline, every quarterly earnings miss feels like a referendum on your portfolio. And yet the true drivers of investment value operate on much slower timescales—product development, brand loyalty, demographic shifts, management culture. These forces do not move on the pace of breaking news. They unfold gradually, and *only investors who resist the illusion of immediacy are positioned to capture their full effect.*

This is why time is not simply a holding period—it is a filter. It clarifies what matters and erodes what doesn't. A business that cannot survive scrutiny over ten years is unlikely to reward you over two. A thesis that dissolves with market turbulence was not built on substance. The longer your horizon, the higher the bar for your decisions—and the lower your exposure to noise. *Patience is not the opposite of urgency. It is the antidote to impulsiveness.*

Even professional investors fall prey to short-termism. Portfolio managers are often judged quarterly. Media personalities are rewarded for bold predictions, not accurate ones. Yet when you examine the track record of institutional capital, it is often the slowest, most boring strategies that outperform. The Yale endowment, under David Swensen, generated superior returns not by making dramatic shifts, but by adhering to an asset allocation model that favoured long-duration thinking and diversification. Their secret was not brilliance. It was clarity.

So how does one build patience—not as a slogan, but as a habit? First, by aligning your investment philosophy with your actual time horizon. If you are investing for retirement twenty years from now, the daily fluctuations in stock prices are not just irrelevant—they are counterproductive distractions. Second, by choosing companies and funds you understand well enough to tolerate during underperformance. You cannot hold what you don't believe in. And belief is not built on hype—it is built on fundamental understanding.

Third, by reframing what it means to win. In investing, the person who looks smartest today is rarely the person who finishes richest tomorrow. Outperformance comes not from acting fast, but from compounding steadily. This is why Buffett describes his favourite holding period as "forever." It's not literal—it's philosophical. It means that *your default posture should be to hold unless the facts change*, not to act unless you're sure.

This is also why so many great investors emphasise temperament over intelligence. Intelligence helps you find good businesses. Temperament allows you to keep them. The market will offer you exit ramps disguised as threats: recessions, corrections, inflation scares, interest rate fears. But the most dangerous events are rarely the ones that make headlines. They are the internal moments of doubt that convince you to abandon a strategy before it has had time to bear fruit.

Even among legendary investors, the returns are rarely smooth. Amazon, one of the most successful stocks of the modern era, dropped more than 90% after the dot-com crash. Apple endured years of stagnation before the iPhone. Netflix was dismissed as a niche DVD delivery service. *Every iconic company has endured periods where it looked like a poor investment.* The question is not whether your holdings will face adversity. The question is whether you will.

Patience is a posture of confidence, not of passivity. It reflects a belief that your decisions are grounded in durable logic. It allows you to zoom out when others are zooming in. It positions you to act strategically, not reactively. And most importantly, it aligns you with the actual mechanics of wealth creation.

There is also an ethical dimension to this. Short-termism incentivises companies to manipulate earnings, reduce investment in R&D, and prioritise quarterly optics over long-term substance. Patient capital, by contrast, gives management the runway to build real value. As a shareholder, you are not just a beneficiary of capitalism—you are a participant in it. Your time horizon shapes the kind of corporate behaviour you endorse.

This is why building a portfolio should begin with a statement of time. Not just how long you intend to hold something, but what you expect of it across that span. Is it a five-year reinvestment vehicle? A twenty-year income generator? A permanent stake in a business you admire? Define it clearly. Then defend it fiercely. Because when markets correct—and they will—that clarity becomes your compass.

To believe in time is to reject the mythology of perfect timing. No one buys at every bottom or sells at every top. Most who try leave money on the table. The irony is that the more you chase precision, the more you sacrifice performance. But when you align with time—when you accept volatility as the cost of admission and compounding as the goal—you liberate yourself from the tyranny of noise.

You cannot control the market. You cannot control the news cycle. But you can control how long you are willing to wait. That control, properly exercised, is the only true edge you will ever need.

Volatility Is Not the Enemy—Misinterpretation Is:

Volatility does not destroy wealth. Behaviour does. When investors speak of risk, they often conflate two distinct phenomena: the temporary fluctuations in asset prices and the permanent loss of capital. The former is volatility—unavoidable, natural, and often irrational. The latter is misjudgement—avoidable, costly, and usually self-inflicted. The distinction is subtle in language but profound in consequence. *Volatility is not your enemy. Misinterpreting it is.*

Markets are noisy by design. Every trade, every uptick, every headline reflects a blend of expectations, speculation, fear, and positioning. It is a dynamic equilibrium shaped less by fundamentals than by narratives, liquidity, and emotion. Yet many investors treat these daily movements as if they contain deep truths—reacting to short-term noise with long-term capital. This is the root of underperformance. *Volatility invites interpretation. Interpretation invites error.*

The modern investor is not lacking information; they are drowning in it. Notifications, charts, economic data releases, analyst opinions, breaking news—all delivered in real time, all demanding a reaction. But the faster the information flows, the harder it becomes to distinguish signal from noise. Signal is what affects long-term value—revenue growth, margin expansion, market share durability, competitive moat, management integrity. Noise is everything else. Most market commentary is not insight—it is distraction dressed in urgency.

Consider a company that announces quarterly earnings. If earnings miss expectations by 3%, the stock may fall 8% the next day. What changed in the business? Perhaps very little. The core product is still profitable. Customers are still loyal. The supply chain is intact. But the consensus estimate—a number constructed from analyst guesses—was not met, and so the market reacts violently. This is volatility driven not by deteriorating fundamentals but by unmet narratives. *The smart investor does not ask, "What did the market expect?" but rather, "Is the business still sound?"*

Misinterpreting volatility as meaningful change is common because the human brain is wired for pattern recognition. We want every price movement to have a reason, every chart to tell a story. But markets often move without logic. A tweet from a central banker. A rumour about tariffs. A shift in interest rate forecasts. These forces can move prices more than a company's actual operations. This is not a flaw in the system—it is its nature. But if you treat every fluctuation as a referendum on your thesis, you will never hold anything long enough to benefit from compounding.

To manage volatility, you must first stop treating it as risk. Volatility is variability, not vulnerability. The volatility of an asset simply measures how far its price deviates over time. A highly volatile asset may experience large swings without any change in intrinsic value. A low-volatility asset, by contrast, may be overvalued but appear stable. *Stability is not safety. Movement is not threat.*

This is why seasoned investors look past the chart and into the cash flow. Is the business generating sustainable earnings? Are margins improving? Is customer retention high? These are signals—grounded in the mechanics of the business, not the mood of the market. The key is to build a process that filters signal from noise, and then to trust that process through volatility. A disciplined checklist, a documented thesis, a regular review cadence—these are not bureaucratic tools. They are cognitive armour.

The temptation to act increases with the speed of information. But clarity does not. Studies in behavioural finance confirm that the more frequently investors check their portfolios, the worse their decisions tend to be. This is known as *myopic loss aversion*—the tendency to overweight short-term losses and underappreciate long-term gains. When you stare at volatility, you begin to feel it viscerally. And once you feel it, your decision-making is no longer analytical—it becomes emotional.

Emotions are not weaknesses. They are evolutionary responses. But they are poorly calibrated for the abstraction of capital markets. Fear, in a biological sense, prompts retreat. But in investing, fear often points to opportunity. A falling price may indicate panic, not deterioration. If you cannot separate your emotional response from the factual condition of the business, you are likely to sell low and buy high. *The enemy is not volatility—it is the meaning you assign to it.*

Take the 2008 financial crisis. During the peak of the sell-off, even high-quality businesses with strong balance sheets saw their share prices cut in half. Investors who interpreted that volatility as a signal of existential collapse locked in losses. Those who understood the underlying fundamentals—and had the temperament to hold—were rewarded handsomely in the recovery. The lesson is not that one should be blind to risk, but that *risk must be defined by business deterioration, not price fluctuation.*

This principle extends to broader market corrections. In early 2020, the COVID-19 pandemic triggered a global sell-off. Indexes plunged. Volatility spiked. Panic was everywhere. But companies like Amazon, Microsoft, and Apple not only weathered the storm—they emerged stronger. Those who sold during the dip missed the compounding rebound. Volatility was loud. Fundamentals were quiet but intact. *The signal was not in the headlines. It was in the balance sheets.*

So how does an investor develop immunity to volatility's deception? First, by reducing exposure to irrelevant noise. Turn off financial television. Stop checking your portfolio daily. Read earnings reports, not Twitter threads. Build your knowledge base around business models, not price targets. Second, by writing down your thesis at the time of purchase. What do you expect from this investment? What would make you sell? What time horizon are you committing to? *Clarity on these questions is your anchor when the winds of volatility pick up.*

Third, by building a system of observation. Review your holdings on a fixed schedule—monthly, quarterly, semi-annually—not in response to price moves. This disciplines your attention and keeps you from reacting impulsively. And finally, cultivate a habit of asking a simple question whenever volatility strikes: *Has anything fundamental changed?* If the answer is no, your default should be to hold.

This mindset is not passive—it is intentional. It takes effort to ignore noise. It takes skill to sit still. But the greatest returns go not to the most active investor, but to the most informed and restrained.

Volatility will never disappear. But your reaction to it can evolve. And that evolution is what separates the trader from the investor, the speculator from the owner.

Ultimately, investing is not about predicting the next move. It is about preparing for the long-term pattern. Volatility will test your nerve. It will shake your thesis. But if you treat it not as a verdict but as a stress test—an opportunity to validate your convictions rather than abandon them—you will navigate it with far greater skill.

The market speaks in noise. But the wise investor listens only for signal.

Building Rituals to Manage Market Anxiety:

Market anxiety is not a flaw in logic—it is a by-product of exposure without insulation. Every investor, no matter how seasoned or systematic, must contend with the emotional undertow of uncertainty. The volatility of asset prices, the stream of financial news, and the ambient hum of economic commentary create an ecosystem wired for overreaction. But anxiety, like volatility, is not inherently destructive. What determines its impact is not its presence, but the discipline with which it is managed. And that discipline is not formed by willpower alone—it is cultivated through ritual.

Rituals are not about superstition or rigidity. They are structured responses to recurring states of uncertainty. They provide scaffolding for thought, creating spaces in which decisions can be made deliberately rather than reactively. In investing, the power of ritual lies in its ability to anchor attention, reduce noise, and foster emotional detachment—not from one's convictions, but from the market's temporary moods. *The antidote to market anxiety is not more information—it is better habits of attention.*

Daily market anxiety is typically driven by exposure to stimuli that offer little insight but demand disproportionate response. The morning financial headlines. The red arrows on a mobile app. The percentage drops of stocks without context. If left unchecked, these fragments produce a constant, low-grade stress—one that corrodes decision quality over time. The first principle of a healthy investing ritual is therefore one of subtraction: limit the frequency and emotional salience of your check-ins.

A practical ritual might begin with a simple rule: *no portfolio checking outside of designated times.* Just as a doctor would not assess a patient's health based on hourly temperature fluctuations, an investor should not measure a portfolio by daily price moves. Pick a consistent window—perhaps late Friday afternoon, after the market closes—and review your holdings once per week. This detachment doesn't signal neglect; it affirms trust in your strategy. The rhythm enforces separation between market noise and personal clarity.

During this weekly check-in, the focus should shift from performance to process. Ask: *Has the business changed, or has the market simply wobbled?* Review earnings reports, industry developments, and strategic news from companies you own. Resist the temptation to react to price alone. If your investment thesis was rooted in fundamentals, then your evaluation should return to fundamentals. This alignment reduces the risk of impulsive decisions disguised as rational pivots.

Quarterly rituals serve a deeper purpose. Unlike the brief pulse check of the weekly review, quarterly rituals offer space for reflection and recalibration. Begin by revisiting your investment journal—the notes, hypotheses, and intentions you documented at the time of purchase. Did the business perform in line with expectations? Were there any structural shifts in the competitive environment? Did management execute on the strategy you found attractive? This reflection transforms investing from an episodic act into a longitudinal inquiry.

It is also during quarterly reviews that you can conduct a structured rebalancing of your portfolio. Not based on recent gains or losses, but on whether your allocations still reflect your goals, risk tolerance, and life context. A younger investor may increase exposure to high-growth equities. A retiree might tilt toward dividend stability. The key is not in the specific action, but in the deliberate cadence with which such decisions are made. *Anxiety shrinks when intention expands.*

The role of rituals is not limited to personal schedule-setting. They also act as safeguards during crisis. During sudden market sell-offs, the absence of structure creates a vacuum—one filled quickly by fear. Investors without predetermined rules often capitulate, selling low out of panic. Those with clear protocols—such as a commitment to hold through 20% drawdowns, or to re-evaluate only after 30 days—are more likely to preserve both capital and clarity. Predefined actions, written in calm, outperform emotional improvisation written in panic.

Beyond the formal rhythms, micro-rituals embedded within your information diet also matter. Choose your sources consciously. Following ten analysts on social media does not make you informed; it makes you scattered. Select a handful of high-quality, long-term focused newsletters, journals, or podcasts. Make them part of your weekly input, not a minute-by-minute feed. And avoid watching the stock ticker like a heart monitor. *What you monitor most, you begin to mistake for meaning.*

Another powerful ritual is silence. Set aside one day a week with zero portfolio interaction. Let the markets move without your attention. Observe your reactions to the absence. The goal is not to become indifferent, but to loosen the compulsive grip of constant vigilance. Investing is an act of ownership, not surveillance. *You are not a security guard—you are a steward of capital.*

Meditative practices, though rarely discussed in financial circles, also have a place in the investor's toolkit. A five-minute breathing exercise before a review session can re-centre focus, reduce cortisol levels, and create cognitive distance from noise. Journaling your emotional state before and after portfolio interactions builds awareness of your psychological triggers. These practices are not ancillary—they are protective. *Markets test your analysis, but they punish your reactivity.*

Crucially, the aim of building rituals is not to eliminate anxiety altogether. That would be unrealistic and, frankly, unwise. Some degree of discomfort is necessary for vigilance and learning. But rituals transform that discomfort into signal. They create containers in which fear can be examined rather than obeyed. And they convert the investor from a passenger of emotion into a pilot of principle.

Consider the example of Charlie Munger, who famously read financial documents daily but rarely traded. His ritual was intellectual, not transactional. Or think of John Templeton, who made investment decisions based on deeply structured quarterly reviews and spiritual detachment. These were not quirks of temperament—they were engineered defences against the emotional sabotage markets provoke. *The calmest investors are rarely the least informed. They are simply the best structured.*

In times of market exuberance, rituals protect against greed. In downturns, they insulate against fear. In stable periods, they reinforce discipline. Regardless of market phase, they create a meta-habit: the habit of treating your behaviour as a controllable variable. You cannot control price movements, interest rate shocks, or geopolitical tremors. But you can control how and when you engage with information. And over time, that control compounds.

Every investor builds a system—intentionally or accidentally. The question is not whether you have rituals. It is whether yours are serving your goals or sabotaging them. Creating a calendar of interaction, a process of review, and a structure of inquiry is not the work of a hobbyist. It is the craft of a professional. And those who treat investing as craft, not entertainment, are the ones most likely to emerge not only with returns—but with peace of mind.

You don't have to be calm to invest well. But you do need systems that make calm possible.

When to Watch, When to Walk Away:

The single most overlooked variable in long-term investing success is not stock selection, asset allocation, or macroeconomic forecasting—it is cadence. How often you engage with your portfolio, and under what mental state, determines whether your returns reflect rational compounding or emotional volatility. This isn't merely a question of discipline; it's one of psychological architecture. Without a defined cadence, your portfolio becomes a mirror of your mood. With one, it becomes a tool of strategy.

There's a seductive illusion that more information equals better outcomes. That watching your investments daily—or even hourly—makes you a more responsible investor. It doesn't. What it makes you is more reactive. The more frequently you monitor your portfolio, the more likely you are to intervene, and most interventions are subtractive rather than additive. Numerous studies confirm this: investors who check less often not only experience less stress, they often achieve better returns, simply by staying out of their own way. *Every glance carries a cognitive cost.*

This doesn't mean detachment is inherently virtuous. The opposite extreme—neglect—can also be damaging. Portfolios untended for years often drift into misalignment: risk profiles change, positions overweight, new life goals emerge unnoticed. The point is not to watch everything, always. It is to *know when to look, and when looking is more dangerous than helpful.*

To design your personal check-in cadence, begin with your temperament. Are you someone who experiences heightened emotional reactions to loss or volatility? Do you tend to act impulsively in the face of uncertainty? If so, your cadence must act as a behavioural circuit-breaker. Limit access. Create friction. Set portfolio review days in advance—say, the last Friday of each month—and avoid any interaction with your brokerage account outside that schedule. Structure protects clarity.

Contrast this with someone who remains largely unemotional and enjoys analysing business fundamentals. For them, a weekly rhythm may be appropriate—*not to track price movement,* but to engage intellectually with developments in the companies they own. In this case, watching is not a trigger for action, but a process of reflection. Cadence, here, enables curiosity without compulsion.

It is essential to distinguish between types of information and the cadence appropriate to each. Price data requires the least frequent review. Fundamentals—such as earnings reports, capital allocation decisions, or regulatory shifts—deserve periodic attention, often quarterly. Your personal life goals—income needs, time horizon, risk capacity—merit reflection perhaps once or twice a year. *Cadence, in this context, becomes layered, not linear.* Not everything should be checked at the same rate.

The problem arises when investors collapse these categories. A small dip in a share price is mistaken for a deterioration in fundamentals. A quarterly earnings miss is misread as a permanent trend. A news story is seen as a signal rather than the noise it usually is. Without cadence, there is no filter. Everything becomes urgent, and urgency is the enemy of patience.

Consider a real-world contrast. Investor A logs into her account daily, reacting to news alerts, Twitter opinions, and market sentiment. She sells a position in a tech company after a 10% drop following a media panic about regulation. Three months later, the stock rebounds after an earnings beat, but she's already moved on. Investor B owns the same company but reviews her holdings monthly, and only in the context of business performance. She notes the regulatory headlines, but her quarterly review shows no change in the underlying business model or cash flow trajectory. She holds. Same data, different cadence, radically different outcome.

Establishing a check-in cadence also reduces cognitive fatigue. Much like a CEO doesn't micromanage every employee every hour but instead relies on periodic reports and structured meetings, the intelligent investor operates at a level of abstraction appropriate to long-term goals. Weekly signal reviews. Quarterly thesis evaluations. Annual strategic alignment. This architecture separates signal from noise and allows thoughtfulness to flourish. *Time is not just a measure of patience—it's a platform for better judgement.*

Technology makes this harder. Your brokerage app doesn't want you to adopt a rational cadence. It wants you engaged constantly. Notifications, red charts, "Top Movers" lists—they're designed for dopamine, not discipline. Designing a cadence, therefore, requires not only scheduling when to look, but engineering your environment to make that schedule possible. Remove price trackers from your home screen. Turn off non-essential alerts. Schedule calendar entries for your reviews and treat them with the same seriousness you would a performance appraisal at work.

Cadence must also be adaptive. During moments of extreme market movement—financial crises, major geopolitical shocks, sector-wide collapses—you may choose to *pause*, rather than *accelerate*, your check-ins. In high-stress environments, the clarity of your thinking diminishes while the cost of errors rises. It is during these periods that walking away becomes an advanced skill. *Disengagement, when purposeful, is not avoidance—it is prudence.*

You also need clarity on *why* you are checking in. Is it to evaluate performance? Update your thesis? Reassess allocations? Or simply out of boredom or anxiety? Most impulsive portfolio interactions stem from the latter. A defined cadence accompanied by a defined purpose makes each engagement more intentional. This is the heart of disciplined investing: aligning frequency of action with quality of thought.

A helpful approach is to treat each check-in as a mini-board meeting. Prepare notes. Articulate your agenda. Document decisions or non-decisions. Keep a journal of your thinking, not just your transactions. Over time, this becomes an archive of your process and a shield against recency bias. When tempted to react, you can consult your prior reasoning, track its evolution, and decide from a position of context rather than impulse.

For longer-term investors, especially those managing retirement accounts or index-heavy portfolios, semi-annual or even annual check-ins may suffice. These reviews focus less on individual positions and more on asset allocation, diversification, and alignment with life goals. Here, the risk isn't missing market opportunities—it's inertia or drift. But even at this slower pace, *cadence still matters.* Without it, rebalancing is forgotten, goals are misaligned, and blind spots grow unnoticed.

There's also a philosophical insight here. *The act of walking away is not a surrender of responsibility—it's an affirmation of your investment philosophy.* It signals trust in the quality of your prior decisions. It reflects the understanding that not every fluctuation demands interpretation, and that silence is often more productive than commentary.

The investor who watches too often becomes a trader by default. The one who never watches becomes a speculator by negligence. The thoughtful investor defines their rhythm and holds to it—regardless of market mood. Because they know that cadence is not just about timing reviews. It is about insulating clarity from chaos, anchoring conviction in structure, and treating attention as a finite resource, to be deployed wisely.

If your goal is to compound wealth, you must also compound calm. Cadence is how you do it. Not by eliminating attention, but by allocating it. Not by reacting, but by returning—on your terms, at your pace, with your philosophy in hand. That is when to watch. That is when to walk away.

Chapter 6
The Lies New Investors Tell Themselves

The most insidious obstacles in investing rarely appear on a ticker—they live quietly in the mind. They are the unspoken narratives, the automatic assumptions, the invisible scripts that shape every financial choice you make. For those just entering the market, these mental scripts are often constructed less from experience than from fear, perfectionism, and misplaced trust. They sound sensible. They even feel protective. Yet they mislead, and all too often, they paralyse. This chapter is not about picking stocks or timing markets—it is about cognitive hygiene. Before wealth can grow externally, clarity must be cultivated internally.

New investors arrive with capital, yes, but also with beliefs—some of them corrosive. Thoughts like "I'll start when I know more," "I lost money, so I must be bad at this," or "I'll just follow what the experts are doing" masquerade as prudence, humility, or logic. In reality, they are often anxiety disguised as reason, discomfort with uncertainty masquerading as wisdom, or avoidance of responsibility dressed as caution. Mastery cannot be achieved while sidestepping friction.

The most persistent psychological barrier is the notion that one must "know more" before acting. It appeals to our academic conditioning: more knowledge must equate to better outcomes. Yet investing is not an exam; it is a craft honed through participation, not perfection. True mastery unfolds iteratively. No amount of reading can simulate the emotional texture of watching your first stock drop 12 per cent in a week. Paradoxically, the investor who starts modestly, with willingness to observe their reactions, often learns faster—and fares better—than the one waiting for a mythical state of readiness. Markets reward practitioners, not perfectionists.

Fear of imperfection intensifies with the first loss. A small drawdown is frequently misread as a verdict on intelligence. The mental leap from "this stock declined" to "I am bad at investing" is rapid and brutal. Yet early losses are not condemnation—they are data, often the most instructive you will encounter. The most capable investors are those who metabolise mistakes constructively. This chapter introduces a framework—the Failure Debrief—for converting emotional sting into intellectual clarity.

Even deliberate self-inquiry can falter if outsourced. The simplicity of copying "experts" is seductive, appearing rational yet undermining growth. Financial TV, influencer stock picks, newsletters filled with "conviction buys"—all create the illusion of insight without rigorous understanding. Learning from others is valuable; mimicking without digesting is intellectual passivity. Conviction cannot be borrowed. Their risk tolerance is not yours; their timeline is not yours; their mistakes will not be reflected in your balance sheet.

One of the most damaging mental habits among novices is the belief that "this time is different." Market euphoria or anxiety always feels unprecedented from within, yet human behaviour rarely changes. Bubbles, panics, booms, crashes—they repeat, donning different costumes but following the same psychological rhythm. Believing in uniqueness during mania or fear fosters impulsivity, prompting investors to abandon what they know in favour of what they hope. Recognising these distortions is vital. Studying market history is not mere academic exercise; it is inoculation against self-deception.

This chapter confronts your investing psychology with honesty and depth. It dissects the narratives that sabotage progress and proposes replacements that are both intellectually sound and actionable. Beyond insight, it cultivates the inner infrastructure essential to long-term investing: resilience, reflection, and responsibility.

You will learn why waiting for perfect understanding is counterproductive, and why small, thoughtful steps into the market teach more than any simulation. Losses, treated properly, become lessons rather than indictments. You will develop a disciplined approach to deconstruct mistakes without internalising them as failure. The instinct to outsource thinking to gurus or pundits will be examined, with guidance for building independent judgement. Finally, you will acquire tools to detect emotional distortions in volatile environments, ensuring temporary euphoria or despair is not mistaken for structural truth.

Each section replaces illusion with grounded insight—insights honed through reflection, tested against history, and sharpened through engagement. Investing is not only a numerical endeavour; it is a practice of the mind. The sooner you interrogate your own narratives, the stronger your financial foundation becomes.

This chapter serves as an intellectual inoculation against the myths that keep newcomers sidelined. It will not prevent mistakes—but it will render you wiser each time you encounter one. Because the most dangerous lies in investing are rarely found in headlines; they are the quiet, persistent stories we tell ourselves, unexamined and unchallenged.

"I'll Start When I Know More"

Among the most enduring myths in personal investing is the belief that knowledge must precede action. It's a seductive idea—grounded in academic instinct, reinforced by caution, and often cloaked in intellectual humility. The investor imagines a future version of themselves who, after reading more, watching enough financial news, or completing yet another course, will finally feel "ready" to act. But investing does not reward intellectual preparedness nearly as much as it rewards behavioural readiness. *What delays most investors is not a lack of knowledge—it is a discomfort with not knowing perfectly.*

Perfectionism in investing is a form of disguised fear. It's not a thirst for competence—it's an aversion to vulnerability. The market, by its nature, refuses certainty. It doesn't offer crystal-clear signals, error-free forecasts, or textbook-perfect scenarios. It offers probabilities, ambiguity, and uncomfortable feedback loops. And yet this is exactly why starting small, imperfectly, and thoughtfully is far more instructive—and far more powerful—than waiting for an imagined state of mastery that will never fully arrive. *Progress in investing is not earned by those who wait to feel smart; it's earned by those willing to feel uncertain—productively.*

Consider this: no amount of theoretical reading prepares a first-time investor for the emotional texture of watching a position decline 15% after purchase. That feeling—the combination of regret, confusion, and self-doubt—cannot be simulated. It must be experienced. And it is precisely through small, real exposures to the market that one begins to develop the emotional muscle memory required for long-term success. Starting small does not mean acting recklessly. It means acting deliberately with limited risk—knowing that experiential learning, especially in finance, compounds faster than passive observation.

There is an asymmetry here that matters. The downside of starting with £200 in a diversified stock is minimal; you may lose a small amount of money. But the upside—the shift in identity from observer to participant, the habits formed around tracking, reflecting, and learning—is enormous. On the other hand, the perceived safety of delay creates its own silent cost: stagnation, loss of time in the market, and the solidification of avoidance patterns. *Waiting feels prudent but rarely is.*

A study of behavioural finance reveals how common this perfectionist mindset is. Researchers from the University of Chicago and Stanford have shown that people consistently overestimate the amount of information required before making a decision, especially in domains tied to personal identity, like investing. This is not rational caution; it is cognitive stalling. Interestingly, investors who took the smallest initial actions—buying a single index fund or contributing modestly to a retirement plan—were far more likely to continue building their portfolio six months later than those who waited to "know more." Starting begets continuation. Waiting often begets more waiting.

The misconception is partly cultural. In most disciplines, competence precedes practice. You don't perform surgery or fly an aircraft until you've undergone rigorous training. But investing is unique—it is one of the few fields where *you must practise in order to develop competence.* No classroom can replicate the iterative calibration that real investing demands. The act of investing—even in small, non-leveraged positions—*is* the training.

Warren Buffett often refers to "learning through owning." He doesn't mean memorising financial ratios in a vacuum. He means buying shares in a business, tracking its quarterly performance, understanding its revenue drivers, and seeing how the market reacts—not just intellectually, but emotionally. Every investor remembers their first few stocks with near-biographical clarity. Not because they were large positions, but because they initiated a shift—from passive learner to active participant. *Ownership is the great accelerator of understanding.*

A powerful thought experiment often reframes this mental block. Ask yourself: if I were required to make a £100 investment today in a company I understand, and I was never allowed to add another pound unless I did so—what would I do? Most people would act. Not because they have perfect knowledge, but because the constraints highlight the value of participation over paralysis. The real barrier is rarely knowledge—it is fear of looking or feeling foolish. But markets do not care how prepared you feel; they care how prepared you behave.

Starting small also helps dissolve the myth of the perfect moment. There is no such thing. The market will never provide an all-clear signal. Economic uncertainty, political noise, valuation debates—they are ever-present. Investing under imperfect conditions is not a flaw; it is the default setting of reality. The more one accepts this, the more one sees waiting for perfection as not just unnecessary—but counterproductive. *Imperfect action creates real feedback. Hesitation creates none.*

Importantly, small starts also limit regret. One of the reasons people hesitate to begin is the fear of getting it wrong. But a £250 mistake in your first stock pick, especially if it leads to a new insight about how you selected that stock, is an investment in your process. Contrast that with someone who spends four years reading and still misses the opportunity to participate in a long-term bull market. *The greatest teacher in investing is not hindsight—it is ownership with accountability.*

There's a broader psychological principle at play here as well. Agency compounds. When people feel in control of their learning, they learn faster. Passive consumption creates the illusion of understanding. Active participation reveals the contours of your blind spots. When you start investing, even modestly, you begin to ask better questions. What drives this company's margins? Why does the market favour growth over dividends in this environment? How should I think about valuation versus momentum? These are not questions that arise from watching YouTube videos—they arise from having something at stake.

This principle applies across domains. No one learns to play the piano by watching others play perfectly. No one becomes a good writer by reading style guides alone. Competence is iterative. Feedback is the real teacher. And the feedback loop in investing begins the moment money meets markets. It is uncomfortable, yes. But it is also the point at which abstract concepts become real. *Starting, not studying, is the inflection point of transformation.*

The final barrier for many is the belief that investing must start with a grand plan. It doesn't. It starts with one account, one decision, and one real stake. From there, you iterate. Complexity can come later. But clarity is what you need to begin. And clarity, paradoxically, is often discovered through action—not preceding it.

There is an elegant symmetry to this truth: markets reward those who move thoughtfully, not those who wait endlessly. Your edge is not your information—it's your ability to make decisions under uncertainty and learn from them faster than others. And that edge is useless if never deployed.

So begin. Begin with £50, £500, or whatever amount makes sense to you. Begin with a company you already understand. Begin with the humility to be wrong and the curiosity to learn why. But begin. Because nothing you read—not even this—will teach you as much as that first real investment.

The investor who begins modestly and early learns faster, builds confidence more organically, and develops habits rooted in reality—not theory. The investor who waits for mastery ensures only that their learning curve remains flat.

"I Lost Money, So I Must Be Bad at This"

No investor escapes unscathed. The idea that one can participate in markets and never lose money is not only naïve—it is actively harmful. It sets an impossible standard and transforms every loss into an indictment of self-worth. But the truth is this: losing money is not a verdict on your intelligence, your talent, or your future as an investor. It is an inevitable part of the process. *The critical distinction is not between those who win and those who lose, but between those who learn and those who retreat.*

The market is not school. In school, failure is a mark against your record. In investing, failure is tuition. You pay in discomfort, doubt, and sometimes dollars—but what you receive in return, if properly examined, is more valuable than any clean record of uninterrupted success. Losses contain embedded insight. They are dense with data. But extracting that value requires a deliberate post-mortem process—one that is analytical without being self-punishing, reflective without being paralysing.

This is where the **Failure Debrief Framework** becomes essential. It is not a script to follow blindly, but a set of disciplined prompts designed to convert pain into pattern recognition. The framework consists of four deceptively simple questions:

1. *What did I expect to happen?*
2. *What actually happened?*
3. *Why was there a difference?*
4. *What would I do differently next time?*

Each question interrupts the emotional narrative that often follows a loss—"I'm terrible at this," "I knew I wasn't cut out for investing," or the most damaging of all: "I'll never try this again." Instead of spiralling into identity-based conclusions, the framework redirects attention to process. It assumes from the outset that the outcome is worth investigating, not internalising.

Take, for instance, the investor who buys shares in a promising tech company that misses earnings estimates and drops 30% in two days. The instinctive response might be embarrassment or anger. But apply the debrief: What was the original thesis? Perhaps the investor expected strong recurring revenue from a new product line. What actually happened? The product underperformed due to unexpected customer churn. Why was there a gap in expectations? Maybe the investor underestimated how crowded the competitive landscape was. And what would change next time? They might realise they failed to study churn metrics or competitive positioning with enough rigour. *Now the loss has yielded a lesson—not just an emotion.*

A market loss is only wasted when it's dismissed or internalised without reflection. The most seasoned investors view losses not as verdicts, but as clues. They study their mistakes the way an engineer studies a structural collapse—not with shame, but with curiosity. What broke? Under what stress conditions? What design flaw went unnoticed?

This posture of inquiry is what separates amateurs from professionals. Professionals do not assume their losses define them. Nor do they blame external forces without critique. They examine their inputs—their research quality, their timing, their conviction, their sizing—and treat every outcome as feedback on their system, not on their identity. *They are not trying to be right—they are trying to get better.*

The temptation to equate losses with personal deficiency runs especially deep for new investors. Much of this is cultural. In most professional settings, mistakes are penalised. You're told to avoid error at all costs. So when a trade or investment turns against you, the conditioned response is shame or retreat. But investing is probabilistic, not deterministic. Even good decisions can lead to bad outcomes in the short term. The only failure that counts is the failure to learn.

There is also a deeper psychological trap at work: *loss aversion.* Behavioural economists such as Daniel Kahneman and Amos Tversky demonstrated that people experience the pain of loss far more intensely than the pleasure of gain. This cognitive bias leads us to catastrophise even small setbacks. A 10% decline on a modest position can feel like a referendum on our abilities. But that reaction is emotional noise—not rational signal.

To offset this bias, seasoned investors build rituals around losses. They document them. They quantify them. They even share them with trusted peers or mentors for external perspective. This creates psychological distance and allows for a more objective analysis. Some of the most successful investment letters—such as those from Howard Marks or the partners at Baillie Gifford—openly dissect failed positions. They don't hide them. They mine them. *Transparency breeds mastery.*

It is also helpful to reframe losses in terms of time, not talent. Most investing losses are not permanent unless you sell at a low without understanding the context. Short-term paper losses are not failures—they are tests of your temperament and process. If you understand why you own something and that thesis remains intact, then a price decline is information—not condemnation.

A useful practice here is to write down your investment rationale at the time of purchase. What did you believe about the company's future? What key metrics were you watching? What timeframe did you envision? Then, when prices fall, you are not scrambling to invent a story in hindsight. You already have a documented thesis to revisit. *This turns a loss into a review—not a panic.*

The greatest investors in history have all lost money—often spectacularly. George Soros misjudged tech valuations. Ray Dalio nearly bankrupted his firm in the early 1980s. Even Warren Buffett, often mythologised for his wisdom, has taken painful hits on airlines, energy companies, and more. What defines these investors is not perfection. It is pattern recognition, humility, and an unshakable commitment to learning.

This is perhaps the most counterintuitive truth in investing: *you will make better decisions not by avoiding pain, but by refining your response to it.* The most valuable insights often come wrapped in discomfort. That discomfort is not evidence you are unqualified—it is evidence you are engaged.

When viewed through this lens, a loss becomes an inflection point. It can either calcify into fear or sharpen into skill. The deciding factor is not the size of the loss, but the quality of the debrief.

The goal is not to eliminate all errors—that's impossible in a probabilistic system. The goal is to eliminate *repeatable* errors. That is the edge of the mature investor. If you misunderstand a business once, that's normal. If you misunderstand the same type of business five times, that's negligence. *Pattern ignorance, not error itself, is the real threat.*

Emotional resilience in investing is built through these cycles. You act, you assess, you adjust. Each loop strengthens your internal decision-making architecture. Over time, losses no longer shake your identity—they inform your craft.

So if you've lost money, welcome. You've entered the real work of investing. The work that begins not with flawless execution, but with reflective iteration. Use it. Write it down. Talk it through. Learn something sharp enough that it changes how you act next time. Because there will be a next time. And what matters most is not that you lost—but that you got wiser.

The best investors are not those who never fall. They are those who build a framework so each fall strengthens the foundation beneath them.

"I'll Just Copy What Experts Do"

At first glance, modelling your investment decisions on the moves of legendary investors seems not just reasonable, but prudent. After all, if Warren Buffett buys Apple, shouldn't you? If Cathie Wood loads up on disruptive tech, why not follow suit? The logic is seductive: shortcut the learning curve by riding the coattails of proven performers. But beneath this strategy lies a dangerous illusion—*the belief that insight can be outsourced, and that conviction can be borrowed.* It cannot.

Following experts without engaging with their reasoning is not investing—it's mimicking. It feels safer because it bypasses uncertainty and self-doubt. But what it actually does is hollow out your decision-making muscles. It substitutes replication for reflection. The result is a portfolio full of other people's ideas, none of which you truly understand, believe in, or are emotionally prepared to hold through volatility. *When markets turn, conviction built on someone else's thesis collapses instantly.*

Consider what happens when a widely followed investor reverses course. A high-profile fund manager trims a position, and retail investors—having followed them in—scramble for the exits, often at a loss. They were never owners of the thesis; they were renters of the reputation. And reputation doesn't shield you from market pain. Worse, many of these expert moves are reported with a delay. By the time their quarterly filings are public, the price may have moved or the rationale may have changed. The window to benefit from their information has likely closed.

The deeper issue, however, is philosophical. Investing is not about arriving at the "right" answer. It's about developing *your* answer. Your tolerance for risk. Your understanding of a business. Your time horizon. A trade that makes sense for a hedge fund running billions in fast-moving capital may be entirely inappropriate for a long-term investor with a modest portfolio and a full-time job. The context is different. The constraints are different. The psychology is different. *Blind imitation ignores all of this nuance and replaces it with a superficial sense of alignment.*

There's also the problem of survivorship bias. We only hear from the experts who are still standing. For every Peter Lynch, there are countless fund managers whose strategies didn't work, whose timing was off, or whose luck ran out. If you're only copying the loudest or most visible names, you're mistaking visibility for reliability. That's not research. That's branding.

None of this is to suggest that expert insight is useless. On the contrary, studying great investors can be profoundly valuable—*if* you approach their work as a set of principles to internalise, not positions to mirror. For instance, reading Howard Marks might help you think more critically about risk. Following Charlie Munger might sharpen your attention to business quality and competitive advantage. These are mental models, not mandates. *The goal is not to clone their portfolios but to cultivate their judgement.*

There is a sharp distinction between inspiration and abdication. Inspiration encourages you to test ideas, to run the numbers, to think independently. Abdication skips that entire process and assumes that because someone else has done the thinking, you don't have to. But conviction without comprehension is fragile. The first serious drawdown will expose the gaps in your understanding—and your confidence.

An example: during the 2020 pandemic market crash, many investors flocked to companies championed by high-profile fund managers. Some did so without evaluating those companies' cash flow, margins, or competitive threats. When prices corrected in 2022 and 2023, many of these investors sold in panic, having never developed a coherent thesis of their own. The experts held or adjusted their positions based on new data. The mimics exited with losses and confusion. *The difference wasn't access to information. It was depth of thought.*

Learning to invest is fundamentally an exercise in *thinking*. It requires that you sit with uncertainty, weigh trade-offs, and develop a personal process for decision-making. This doesn't mean isolating yourself from wisdom. It means engaging with it actively. Ask yourself: What is this expert seeing that I'm not? What assumptions are they making? Would I have made the same call if I were unaware of their reputation? What part of this thesis resonates with my own analysis—and what part raises doubt?

This practice builds what psychologists call *cognitive independence*—the ability to reason through complex choices without defaulting to authority. In investing, this is a crucial survival skill. No one else can hold your portfolio through a downturn. No one else feels your fear, your goals, your trade-offs. Delegating decisions might feel easier, but it leaves you unprepared for adversity. *Your portfolio reflects your thinking—or someone else's.*

A more effective approach is to treat expert activity as a prompt, not a prescription. If you notice that a seasoned investor is buying a particular stock, don't buy it blindly. Study it. Reverse-engineer their thinking. Read the company's filings. Understand its revenue model, cost structure, strategic risks, and potential catalysts. Think through scenarios—bullish and bearish—and decide whether you believe the business deserves your capital. If you reach the same conclusion, fine. But it must be *your* conclusion.

This process takes time. It is slower than mimicry. It does not yield immediate confidence. But over time, it builds something far more powerful: *conviction born of comprehension.* When volatility strikes, you won't be asking, "What is the expert going to do?" You'll be asking, "Has anything fundamentally changed in the business I understand?" That shift is transformative.

There is also an ethical component to this discussion. Many of the experts you might follow have dramatically different incentives from your own. Fund managers are often rewarded based on short-term relative performance. Their risk tolerance, position sizing, and turnover are dictated by institutional mandates. They may be managing money for pension funds or sovereign wealth entities. You are managing money for your future, your family, your freedom. *The stakes are personal—and that demands personal accountability.*

In practical terms, this means building your own investment checklist. Document the criteria that matter most to you—perhaps it's a sustainable competitive advantage, consistent free cash flow, strong insider ownership, or moderate debt. Then evaluate every opportunity—regardless of who recommends it—against that checklist. This is how you build internal consistency and avoid lurching between styles, sectors, or timeframes depending on the expert of the month.

Resisting the urge to copy also helps you develop a deeper relationship with uncertainty. Markets don't reward certainty—they reward thoughtful risk-taking. The sooner you abandon the fantasy of perfect information and realise that all investing involves probabilities, the faster you will begin to cultivate real skill. *Copying delays this growth because it tricks you into thinking you're investing when you're merely echoing.*

To be clear, learning from experts is invaluable. But *learning from* is different from *leaning on.* One cultivates strength. The other breeds dependence. The investor who develops their own views—

tempered by outside insight but forged in personal analysis—will always have a stronger foundation than the one who merely follows others.

So by all means, read the letters, listen to the interviews, study the trades. But use them as sandpaper for your own thinking—not scaffolding to prop up a weak thesis. Because when the market tests your conviction—and it will—the only compass that matters is the one you built yourself.

The best investors are not those who follow the best ideas. They are those who learn how to generate their own.

"This Time Is Different"

Few phrases have proven more expensive than "this time is different." It is the four-word rationale that has justified some of the most catastrophic asset bubbles in history. Not because it's always wrong in the narrowest sense—technological, political, and financial contexts do evolve—but because it often blinds investors to the one thing that remains reliably constant: *human behaviour*. Greed, fear, euphoria, denial, and regret play out in cycles that transcend industries and generations. The illusion of difference is seductive. The reality of repetition is instructive.

To understand why this phrase persists, you have to recognise that it rarely emerges during calm or sceptical periods. It surfaces during extremes—when prices surge, when narratives compound, when doubters are ridiculed and believers appear visionary. In those moments, calling back to historical precedent feels not just inconvenient but naive. Why look backward when everyone else is charging forward? The problem is that these cycles—however novel they seem on the surface—are emotionally identical under the skin.

Take the dot-com bubble of the late 1990s. The internet was, indeed, a transformative technology. It *did* change commerce, communication, and culture. But the narrative of unbounded potential led to valuations that detached from basic financial realities. Companies with no revenue were priced as if they would dominate trillion-dollar markets. As Nasdaq soared past 5,000, sceptics were told they "didn't get it." When the bubble burst, those who had ignored basic metrics—like profitability or path to sustainability—paid the price. What felt different in the moment was, in fact, the same pattern that fuelled the South Sea Bubble in 1720 or the Nifty Fifty boom in the 1970s: *a compelling story, uncritical optimism, and eventually, a painful reckoning.*

More recently, the cryptocurrency boom of 2017, and again in 2021, followed a strikingly similar trajectory. Blockchain technology may well be revolutionary. But the frenzy around coins, tokens, and NFTs escalated faster than most participants understood. The line between innovation and speculation blurred. Retail investors poured in not because they understood distributed ledger architecture, but because prices were going up and others were getting rich. Once again, fundamentals took a backseat to FOMO. And once again, when the correction came, many were left with assets they didn't truly understand and losses they didn't anticipate.

The emotional logic behind "this time is different" is rooted in *narrative overconfidence.* When something feels unprecedented—because it involves a new technology, a charismatic founder, a generational shift—it becomes easy to convince ourselves that old rules no longer apply. Price-to-earnings ratios? Irrelevant. Debt loads? Obsolete. Competitive moats? A relic of the industrial age. The rational mind defers to the fevered market, and prudent scepticism is rebranded as cynicism or fear-mongering.

The antidote is not to become a perma-sceptic or to dismiss all innovation. The antidote is *pattern recognition.* Noticing that, regardless of asset class or economic context, markets have always gone through cycles of exuberance and despair. Recognising that hype tends to peak when it becomes socially uncomfortable to disagree. And accepting that discipline in the face of narrative euphoria is a learned skill—*one that separates sustainable investors from speculative tourists.*

It's important to note that not all bubbles are entirely irrational. Many begin with a kernel of truth. The electric vehicle revolution is real. So is the increasing power of artificial intelligence. But truth is not the same as valuation discipline. What starts as reasonable optimism can quickly mutate into careless extrapolation. Tesla may have pioneered a shift in transportation, but at various points its valuation implied world domination. Nvidia's leadership in GPUs is profound, but even good companies can become overpriced if expectations grow faster than execution. *Understanding the business is necessary; understanding the sentiment surrounding it is equally vital.*

This brings us to the distinction between hype cycles and price bubbles. A hype cycle refers to the narrative energy driving investor behaviour. A price bubble refers to the numeric detachment from intrinsic value. You can have one without the other—briefly. But when both converge, risk multiplies. Spotting a hype cycle involves more than watching CNBC or monitoring trending tickers. It means asking hard questions: What assumptions are embedded in today's price? What would need to happen—in revenue, margins, adoption rates—for this valuation to be justified? Who is buying, and why?

A useful framework here is what some analysts call *narrative velocity*. If a stock or sector is moving faster in media coverage than in fundamental development, that's a warning sign. If the CEO is on magazine covers more than they are in earnings calls, pause. If the justification for holding an asset relies more on social consensus than financial logic—"Everyone knows this is the future"—then you're operating in the realm of belief, not analysis.

Psychologically, humans are bad at scaling exponential change. We anchor to linear models. When we see rapid growth, we project it forward uncritically. A company doubling revenue for three years straight seems unstoppable—until competition, saturation, or regulation enters the picture. The idea that "this time is different" often stems from extrapolation without friction. A belief that winners will keep winning, that multiples will keep expanding, that demand will keep surging. History warns otherwise.

The irony is that even seasoned investors fall into this trap. Ray Dalio, Jeremy Grantham, and others have admitted to missing major moves or being caught in consensus errors. Intelligence is not immunity. If anything, smarter investors may be more susceptible to overfitting a narrative to confirm their views. The defence is not superior intellect but structured doubt—a habit of asking: *What would I need to see to change my mind?*

Teaching yourself to recognise hype requires intentional practice. One technique is to keep a *Sentiment Journal*—a record of how people are talking about particular stocks, sectors, or strategies. Not what the data says, but what the mood feels like. Are media headlines euphoric or anxious? Are investors calm or tribal? Is disagreement possible without being shouted down? These subtle signals often provide an early read on emotional overheating.

It also helps to revisit market history with curiosity, not nostalgia. Study not just the mechanics of crashes, but the psychology that preceded them. Read primary sources—investor letters, newspaper headlines, analyst notes—from the months before major corrections. What were people saying in 1929, 2000, or 2008? You'll notice eerie similarities: phrases like "new paradigm," "once-in-a-generation opportunity," or "markets are simply more efficient now." Different eras. Same illusions.

To be clear, innovation should not be feared. But it should be priced with sobriety. Investing in emerging technologies or disruptive firms can be a smart part of a diversified strategy—*if* you know what you're buying and why. But buying based on narrative momentum alone is not a strategy. It's a sentiment trade dressed up in buzzwords.

The phrase "this time is different" is not merely a cliché—it's a psychological defence mechanism. It allows investors to suspend critical thinking in favour of social comfort. It's easier to be wrong with the crowd than right in isolation. But investing is not a popularity contest. Your job is not to agree with consensus but to *think independently enough to protect your capital when consensus unravels.*

Ultimately, recognising the emotional cycles of markets is as important as understanding the financial ones. It's not enough to analyse the business—you must also analyse the behaviour surrounding the business. Because while technologies change, policies shift, and macro environments evolve, *the way humans respond to hope, fear, and money remains astonishingly consistent.* That is the real cycle worth mastering. And it's never different.

Chapter 7
The Skeleton of a Sound Portfolio

A portfolio is not merely a collection of stocks; it is a carefully constructed framework, an architecture of intention that embodies your beliefs, temperament, priorities, and appetite for risk. It is not a catalogue of past decisions nor a display of the market's current favourites. Rather, it is a living system whose design deserves scrutiny as rigorous as the analysis applied to individual holdings. Resilience in investing is rarely born of prediction; it arises from preparation. And that preparation begins with structure—deliberate construction of conviction, not the pursuit of performance alone.

Far too often, novices equate diversification with accumulation. Owning twenty securities with overlapping industry, geographic, or economic exposures is not diversification—it is duplication masquerading as prudence. True diversification spreads risk across different vectors: business models, sectors, currencies, and regulatory regimes. It demands an understanding of potential failure as much as of potential success, along with the humility to acknowledge that not every component will lead at all times.

This humility underpins the core-satellite model. Consider it skeletal engineering: the core is your spine—stable, unassuming, enduring. Core holdings anchor your portfolio: broad market funds, global equity ETFs, or mature companies selected for durability rather than dazzle. Surrounding that spine are satellites—smaller, agile allocations that allow thematic bets, experimental ideas, or personal expression. This dual structure balances two psychological imperatives: the need for disciplined stability and the desire for engagement. It honours past analysis without imprisoning you to it and permits evolution without collapse.

The challenge is weight. Too heavy a core and your portfolio may lag innovation; too prominent a satellite and volatility may outpace reward. That balance should emerge from conviction, not templates or internet forums. If you hold something because a podcast praised it, or because it has been green on your screen for weeks, you are outsourcing your thinking. A robust portfolio reflects your synthesis of knowledge and insight, not imitation.

Conviction differs from confidence. Confidence is fleeting and emotional; conviction is the product of research, reflection, and rational synthesis. It has little to do with charisma or the appeal of a CEO's narrative. It develops over time through fundamental analysis, pattern recognition, and clarity of thesis. A portfolio rooted in conviction evolves with evidence, not headlines. It is guided by reasoned judgement rather than impulse or sentiment.

Rebalancing is another frequently misunderstood principle. It is not a mechanism for chasing performance; it is risk management in action. Rebalancing requires selling what has outperformed and buying what has lagged, not to time markets, but to preserve the portfolio's intended structure. Too often, investors interpret this act as doubt or as a market call. Done correctly, it is a reaffirmation of strategy: a commitment to principles over panic, to logic over emotion.

Drift is unavoidable. Markets rotate, sectors surge or falter, and individual positions fluctuate. Without deliberate attention, your carefully designed allocation becomes unrecognisable. Rebalancing is not mere bookkeeping—it is philosophical: a moment to ask, "Does this still reflect my beliefs?"

Simplicity scales. Complexity often masquerades as sophistication, yet the more intricate a portfolio, the harder it is to monitor, evaluate, and maintain consistency. Complexity without purpose invites errors under pressure. Clarity, not convolution, is the armour during market stress. Every holding must serve a purpose, and every purpose should be traceable to a reasoned thesis revisited with intellectual honesty.

Your portfolio is a mirror. It reflects not only your financial goals but your psychology—discipline, temperament, and worldview. Are you deliberate or reactive? Guided by reason or by fear of missing out? Do you trust cycles, fundamentals, or narratives? The structure of your holdings exposes these truths more candidly than questionnaires ever could.

Constructing a sound portfolio is therefore as much about resilience as returns. You will not always select the top performer, and that is acceptable. If the architecture is strong—anchored in principles, not predictions—success follows from patience and consistency rather than perfect foresight. Avoid ruin, harness compounding, and remain in the game; the logic of your decisions will assert itself over time.

This chapter equips you to distinguish core from satellite holdings, to grasp diversification in its truest sense, and to invest with conviction rather than convenience. You will learn when, why, and how to rebalance strategically, and how to build a system that respects uncertainty while aligning with your evolving priorities.

In short, a portfolio is more than a set of assets—it is a framework of thought, a reflection of judgment, and a vessel for endurance. Its structure, rationale, and your composure amid chaos define its ultimate success. This is the essence of a resilient portfolio, and it is what separates hopeful investors from those who endure.

Core, Satellite, and the Art of Simplicity:

If most people treated their investments the way they treat their wardrobes, the results would be catastrophic. Imagine owning a chaotic mix of garments, purchased on impulse, few of which fit well, serve a consistent function, or reflect the life you actually live. This, in effect, is how many portfolios are built: an accumulation of ideas, headlines, and hot tips, lacking both structure and clarity. The remedy is not complexity—it is intentional design. And among the most enduring frameworks for structuring a sound, manageable portfolio is the core-satellite model: a two-layer approach that combines *simplicity with flexibility*, *discipline with curiosity*.

At its essence, the core-satellite strategy does something psychologically profound. It separates the serious from the speculative. It carves out a space for long-term, stable holdings—the "core"—while giving permission for exploration through smaller, tactical positions—the "satellites". This structure allows investors to avoid two common traps: overconfidence, which leads to reckless concentration, and over-diversification, which dilutes conviction into noise.

The core is where clarity lives. It is the financial equivalent of bedrock: broad-based, dependable, low-maintenance. Think global equity ETFs, diversified index funds, or a carefully selected set of high-quality companies with consistent earnings, defensible moats, and proven management. These are the holdings that you intend to own for a decade or more—not because they're exciting, but because they are enduring. The role of the core is not to outperform in any given quarter, but to *compound reliably* over long horizons.

A well-constructed core offers four invaluable traits: exposure, efficiency, predictability, and peace of mind. It reflects your central investment beliefs and acts as a ballast when markets grow turbulent. Importantly, it also limits the emotional bandwidth spent on constant decision-making. When the bulk of your portfolio is anchored in logic and stability, the urge to react to headlines or short-term volatility is meaningfully reduced.

But humans are not spreadsheets. We are narrative-driven, future-curious creatures. We enjoy engaging with ideas, trends, and the unfolding of possibilities. This is where the satellite component earns its place. A satellite holding is a smaller, focused allocation—perhaps to a high-growth company, a niche thematic ETF, or an under-the-radar emerging market. Its purpose is not to anchor, but to explore. It allows you to express a view, test an insight, or lean into a thesis—*without endangering the integrity of the whole portfolio.*

Crucially, the satellite layer is not an excuse for gambling. It must still be governed by thoughtful entry criteria, risk limits, and exit conditions. If a satellite position becomes too large—or dominates your attention—it has outgrown its role. The point is to contain volatility, not import it into the core. An effective metaphor is to think of the core as your house, and satellites as seasonal projects in the garden. You maintain them, enjoy them, and sometimes experiment with them—but you don't sleep in them during a storm.

One of the underappreciated advantages of the core-satellite structure is that it respects *investor temperament.* Some people are deeply risk-averse. Others are fascinated by innovation and disruption. Rather than suppress either impulse, this model channels both: the core enforces rationality, while the satellites indulge curiosity in measured doses. It acknowledges that discipline and play can coexist—so long as they are proportionate and deliberate.

What proportion makes sense? There is no universal answer, but as a general guide, the core should represent *at least* 70–80% of your total equity exposure. Satellites should be the minority—not because they're unimportant, but because they're inherently more volatile and less predictable. If a satellite thesis succeeds, it adds spice to your returns. If it fails, it doesn't sink the ship. This balance allows you to learn, adjust, and evolve—without putting your financial future at risk.

Let's ground this in a practical example. Consider an investor in her early thirties with a stable income, long time horizon, and an interest in emerging technologies. Her core might consist of low-cost global index funds, supplemented by a few large-cap dividend growers and inflation-linked bonds. That provides diversification, income stability, and low-cost compounding. Her satellites, meanwhile, could include a modest allocation to clean energy stocks, a position in a cybersecurity ETF, and a small speculative stake in a biotech startup. The structure protects her from concentration risk while still letting her participate in innovation. It is a portfolio designed not just for returns—but for *resilience and engagement.*

Contrast this with a common pitfall: the "accidental portfolio". Built over years of disconnected decisions, it lacks a unifying framework. Some stocks are held out of nostalgia, others out of habit, and many are leftovers from a fleeting conviction. There is no architecture—only accumulation. When market turbulence hits, such a portfolio offers little clarity about what to hold, what to cut, or what role each asset plays. The investor feels disoriented because the portfolio itself is disoriented. The core-satellite model prevents this drift. It demands that every position earn its place.

There's also an elegance to its simplicity. Rather than chasing endless diversification, the model teaches you to *diversify by design.* You are not spreading across more names for the sake of it—you are allocating based on function and conviction. The core ensures exposure to broad market progress. The satellites ensure alignment with your unique worldview, interests, or research edge. Together, they form a portfolio that is both personal and principled.

This approach also scales over time. As your wealth grows, the structure remains relevant. A young investor might start with a simple 80% global index fund, 20% thematic ETF mix. Over time, that core can evolve into a blend of direct equity holdings, infrastructure exposure, or sector-specific funds—while still keeping the logic intact. The satellite portion can rotate as interests or macro views shift. You are not forced to rebuild your portfolio from scratch every few years. You're simply updating the modules within a well-constructed framework.

Of course, no structure eliminates the need for judgement. A satellite can become a core candidate if conviction deepens and fundamentals strengthen. Likewise, a core holding can be downgraded if its thesis decays. But the framework *forces these decisions to be intentional.* You are constantly asking: Is this a foundational belief, or a temporary thesis? Is this worth 15% of my net worth—or 2% of my experimental allocation? These are not academic questions. They are the difference between a robust portfolio and a fragile one.

Ultimately, the core-satellite model is a philosophy of *deliberate simplicity*. It accepts that the market is unpredictable, that investors are emotional, and that no amount of tinkering can eliminate risk. What it offers instead is clarity. It enables you to build something that lasts—not because it's perfect, but because it's *coherent.* It lets you navigate uncertainty without being paralysed by it. And it gives you the confidence that comes from knowing exactly *why* you own what you own.

That clarity is rare. In a world of financial noise, where apps, influencers, and market pundits clamour for your attention, a well-designed portfolio is a quiet act of resistance. It says: I don't need to chase. I have a system. I trust my process. And I've built something I can live with—through the highs, the lows, and everything in between.

This is the art of simplicity, not as minimalism, but as precision. It's not about owning less. It's about owning *with purpose.* And that is what makes the core-satellite structure not just a technique—but a foundational skill of the thoughtful investor.

Diversification: More Than a Buzzword:

It is one of the most repeated mantras in modern investing: "Diversify." But repetition does not equate to comprehension. Too often, diversification is treated as a checkbox activity—a surface-level exercise in owning more stocks, adding more tickers, or buying into another fund. The belief is that breadth equals safety, and that quantity is a proxy for risk management. Yet the reality is more subtle—and far more consequential. *True diversification is not about having more investments; it's about having different exposures.* Different behaviours under stress. Different economic sensitivities. Different reasons to rise or fall.

The danger of mistaking variety for true diversification is not merely theoretical. It becomes painfully visible in times of crisis. Take March 2020. As the COVID-19 pandemic rattled markets globally, many portfolios that appeared diverse on paper revealed their hidden correlations. Investors holding "diversified" baskets of US tech, high-growth European equities, and emerging market internet stocks soon discovered that they had simply made variations on a single bet: momentum-fuelled, growth-oriented risk assets. When fear surged, they all moved in tandem—down. This phenomenon wasn't new. It echoed what occurred in 2008, when ostensibly diversified portfolios crumbled because most holdings were tied, directly or indirectly, to credit expansion.

To understand diversification properly, one must first abandon the simplistic view of it as an arithmetic problem. It's not a matter of how many holdings you own—it's about *what those holdings are exposed to.* Think in terms of economic drivers, behavioural patterns, and structural incentives. A UK energy giant, a Japanese robotics manufacturer, and a Brazilian agricultural firm might all sit in your portfolio—but if they are each dependent on the same commodity cycle or global demand surge, you are not diversified in any meaningful way. You are simply spread.

This distinction is critical. Diversification is not dilution. A well-diversified portfolio is not one that holds everything—it is one that holds *enough of the right things to prevent any one scenario from dominating your future.* It is a protection against narrative traps, geographic biases, and sectoral overcommitment. It is also, at its best, a protection against your own conviction bias—the tendency to overestimate what you know and underestimate what you can't imagine.

Let's drill deeper into what makes diversification real. The first axis is **industry independence**. Sectors behave differently under varying macroeconomic conditions. Utilities tend to remain relatively stable through economic slowdowns; they provide essential services, often with regulated pricing. Technology, on the other hand, is inherently pro-cyclical—when economic optimism wanes, spending on software, hardware, and innovation contracts. Healthcare might exhibit resilience during downturns but may face regulatory scrutiny in election years. A portfolio concentrated in only one or two of these sectors may thrive during a specific phase of the cycle, but will inevitably suffer during another. True diversification spreads risk across these differing cycles—not based on popularity or recent returns, but based on function.

The second axis is **geographic exposure**. It's easy to assume that large-cap multinational companies offer sufficient global reach. After all, companies like Nestlé, Apple, or Toyota generate revenues from dozens of countries. But revenue exposure is not the same as jurisdictional independence. Regulatory risk, currency fluctuations, capital controls, tax policy shifts—these are location-dependent risks that even global firms cannot fully escape. Holding assets across geographies—through direct international equities, regional ETFs, or global funds with genuinely uncorrelated mandates—can buffer your portfolio against localised political shocks or economic stagnation. It also helps hedge against the fallacy of national exceptionalism—the belief that one country, however stable or innovative, is forever immune to crisis.

The third and often neglected dimension is **business model diversity**. This means owning companies or funds that make money in fundamentally different ways. Consider an online retailer and a logistics firm. Both may rise in a bullish consumer environment, but their economic engines are distinct: one monetises attention and transactions; the other monetises scale and infrastructure. Similarly, a software-as-a-service company relies on subscription renewals and digital lock-in, while a mining operation extracts value from physical depletion. Business models shape risk profiles. They determine cost structures, sensitivity to inflation, capital intensity, and strategic flexibility. A diversified portfolio includes not just different names—but different *ways of winning and surviving.*

Yet diversification is not only an analytical exercise—it's a psychological one. Investors often fail to diversify not because they don't understand the theory, but because they don't trust it. They chase familiarity, stories, and performance. Home bias—overinvesting in one's own country—is a persistent problem even in mature markets. So is recency bias—overweighting whatever has done well in the last five years. This is how portfolios drift into concentration without any formal decision being made. Diversification requires intentionality. It is an act of humility. It says: *I cannot know the future. Therefore, I must prepare for more than one version of it.*

It also demands trade-offs. True diversification dilutes the upside as well as the downside. It means being willing to underperform the best asset class or trend of the year. That is the price of resilience. When the world is booming, a diversified portfolio can feel frustratingly ordinary. But when dislocation hits—when correlations collapse and volatility spikes—it is the difference between a bruise and a blow.

The value of diversification is best appreciated across decades, not days. Consider the portfolios of long-term endowments, such as Yale or Harvard. Their returns are not driven by a handful of stock picks, but by thoughtful allocation across global equities, real assets, private markets, fixed income, and alternatives—balanced by risk, liquidity needs, and return targets. Their strategies are not built to maximise return in the next quarter; they are designed to persist, adapt, and survive across regimes.

Modern technology makes diversification easier than ever—but also more deceptive. The rise of ETFs has democratised access to sectors and geographies, but it has also created a false sense of safety. Buying five ETFs does not guarantee diversification if they all track similar indices or respond to the same economic inputs. Many ETFs are derivatives of the same underlying exposure. Owning a Nasdaq 100 ETF, a US technology ETF, and a "future innovation" thematic fund might look like diversification—but in a downturn, they may all fall together. What matters is *correlation*, not category.

So how should the thoughtful investor approach diversification in practice? Start with clear thinking about what you're protecting against: inflation spikes, currency devaluation, regulatory shocks, recessions, technological disruption, geopolitical instability. Then ask: what assets behave differently under those conditions? Diversify not by surface, but by substance.

There is also a critical role for *self-awareness*. Some investors thrive on simplicity—owning a global equity tracker and rebalancing once a year. Others enjoy crafting bespoke portfolios across asset classes and regions. Both approaches can be valid—*if the underlying exposures are truly differentiated.* The key is that diversification is not a goal in itself. It is a method of risk-aware positioning. It's about building a portfolio that is strong not because every part always works, but because *not every part fails at once.*

Finally, diversification is not static. The world evolves. Correlations change. Economic regimes rotate. What diversified your portfolio ten years ago may not do so tomorrow. This is why periodic review is essential—not frantic rotation, but strategic assessment. Diversification is not a destination. It is a discipline. And when done with care, it becomes more than a buzzword. It becomes your portfolio's deepest form of self-defence.

Your Portfolio as a Reflection of Conviction:

If someone looked at your portfolio without knowing you personally, would they be able to guess what you believe in—about the world, the markets, risk, or opportunity? Or would they see only a scattered collage of ticker symbols cobbled together from headlines, advice, and market noise? This is not a theoretical question. It goes to the heart of intelligent investing. *A portfolio, at its best, is a mirror of conviction—not just a reflection of current trends or market capitalisations.* And building one that accurately reflects what you believe is not just more meaningful—it is more sustainable.

Modern portfolio construction often encourages a mechanical approach. Allocate by region. Allocate by sector. Allocate by asset class. Fill the boxes. Rebalance quarterly. The result may appear diversified, structured, and efficient. But too often, it lacks soul. It lacks intention. And crucially, it lacks asymmetry—because in real life, we do not believe all opportunities are equal. Some businesses seem clearly more resilient, some technologies more transformative, some macro risks more imminent. Yet many investors default to equal weighting or index mirroring, not because they agree with the distribution, but because they fear being wrong in public. *Conviction, by contrast, is the willingness to act on differentiated belief—measured, tested, but not neutralised by consensus.*

The challenge, of course, is that conviction must be earned. It cannot be copied or borrowed. Following what others believe without understanding why is not conviction; it is mimicry. And mimicry tends to unravel under pressure. When a stock declines and your reason for owning it was someone else's confidence, panic follows. But if your thesis was grounded in research, reflection, and deliberate assessment, you are more likely to respond with poise—re-evaluate, yes, but not abandon out of emotion.

This is why the act of *weighting* matters just as much as the act of *selecting*. What you include in your portfolio is one layer of expression. How much you allocate to it is another. A single-digit exposure to an idea might signal mild interest. A 20% allocation speaks to strong belief. And a concentrated bet—when used judiciously—can signal a differentiated insight. This is not a call for recklessness. It is a reminder that weighting is not neutral. *Every portfolio tells a story, and if all positions are treated equally, that story becomes incoherent.*

Consider some examples. An investor who believes deeply in global decarbonisation might express that through heavy weighting in clean energy infrastructure, rare earth miners, and carbon credit ETFs—not just a token ESG fund. Someone who sees geopolitical tension as a long-term driver of supply chain realignment might favour logistics firms, regional manufacturing hubs, and defence stocks. Another who trusts that human creativity remains underpriced may lean into gaming, IP-heavy entertainment, or AI-enablement platforms. Conviction-based investing does not mean narrowness; it means intentionality.

That said, conviction is not binary. It is not simply "I believe in this" or "I don't." It exists on a spectrum. And managing that spectrum intelligently is a learned skill. One of the most practical tools is what could be termed *belief-tiered allocation.* This approach maps positions across three levels:

1. **High-conviction anchors** – ideas where you've done deep research, tested the counterarguments, and have confidence in the long-term fundamentals. These earn larger allocations—often 10% or more of the portfolio—and represent the backbone of your strategy.
2. **Moderate-conviction exposures** – ideas you find promising but are still watching evolve. These might receive mid-sized allocations and are subject to further review or strengthening of thesis over time.
3. **Low-conviction experiments** – areas of curiosity or thematic bets you wish to learn more about. These are deliberately sized small—1–3%—with clear exit criteria or evaluation checkpoints.

This tiered structure allows you to express belief while containing risk. It also creates a feedback loop: as your understanding deepens, ideas can graduate from experimental to core. Or, when a thesis weakens or a narrative shifts, a high-conviction position can be downgraded rather than defended irrationally. *A conviction-based portfolio is not static—it is alive, evolving with the evidence, and responsive to new information without being reactive to noise.*

Another underappreciated insight is that conviction is not the same as overconfidence. True conviction comes with humility. It recognises that belief strength should be proportionate to evidence, not ego. Investors often get this backwards. They allocate based on enthusiasm, not probability. This is where structured thinking, scenario modelling, and rigorous journaling can sharpen conviction while keeping it grounded. The question should not be "How much do I like this company?" but "How strong is the case relative to the risk, and what would make me change my mind?"

In this sense, your portfolio is not just an expression of beliefs—it is a learning tool. Every position becomes a hypothesis being tested in real time. If you treat each asset not as a trophy, but as a thesis, you begin to invest like a researcher: open-minded, hypothesis-driven, and focused on refining insight rather than proving yourself right.

Let's take this further. Think about the classic 60/40 portfolio—60% equities, 40% bonds. For decades, this has been the default model for retail and institutional investors alike. But does it reflect the conviction of the average modern investor? Likely not. In a low-interest-rate, high-inflation, tech-driven world, many investors express deep belief in non-traditional assets—crypto, private equity, infrastructure, thematic ETFs, or global small caps. Yet they default back to a legacy model out of convention or inertia. If your portfolio does not reflect the world as you see it evolving—or the risks you feel are being underpriced—you are outsourcing your worldview to someone else's template.

Of course, conviction must coexist with diversification. These are not competing principles. A thoughtful portfolio balances strong views with hedged humility. Concentrated where belief is earned, spread where uncertainty is acknowledged. That is how seasoned investors operate. They don't dilute every idea to the same size in the name of safety. Nor do they pile recklessly into a single winner. They curate a mosaic—carefully weighted, thoughtfully built, personally resonant.

This approach demands discipline. It requires that you articulate your thesis in writing, test it against disconfirming data, and revisit it with fresh eyes over time. It also requires emotional regulation. Conviction without emotional maturity quickly turns into stubbornness. The best investors are not the most opinionated. They are the most *clear-headed* about which opinions deserve action—and how much of their capital those opinions truly merit.

Ultimately, the portfolio is a personal statement. Not in the sense of ego or branding, but in the sense of self-awareness. It reflects how you see risk, what you think matters, and where you believe value is mispriced. A generic portfolio might earn market returns, but it teaches you very little. A conviction-based portfolio, on the other hand, becomes a teacher. It pushes you to think harder, learn faster, and act with integrity—not to trends, but to your own evolving framework.

So when you next review your holdings, don't just ask: What do I own? Ask: *What does this say about what I believe—and do the allocations match the strength of those beliefs?* If not, you're not investing from conviction. You're just spectating with money on the line.

Rebalancing Without Panic:

If there is a single behavioural error that silently erodes long-term portfolio performance, it is not failing to predict the future correctly. It is overcorrecting in the present unnecessarily. Rebalancing—adjusting the weightings of assets in a portfolio—is often framed as a purely rational task. But beneath the surface, it is a deeply psychological event. *It tests your ability to act in alignment with principles, not emotions.* And if you don't have clearly defined principles, you will inevitably act on vibes.

At first glance, rebalancing sounds straightforward. Stocks have risen, bonds have lagged—trim the former, top up the latter, return to target weights. But in the moment, when equity valuations are stretched and headlines are euphoric, it feels counterintuitive to sell the very assets that are performing well. The opposite is also true. When markets plunge, and certain sectors are hammered, rebalancing requires you to buy what feels broken. In both cases, *the act of rebalancing is not about forecasting the next move—it is about reaffirming the structure you designed before emotion entered the room.*

The problem is that few investors design that structure thoughtfully. Most cobble together allocations based on general guidelines, vague trends, or the latest advice. When turbulence hits, they lack an anchor. So they ask the wrong question: *"What do I feel like doing?"*

rather than *"What does my strategy require of me right now?"* This is the root of panic rebalancing—overreacting to volatility, abandoning allocations without process, and shifting based on discomfort instead of signal.

The antidote is not automation. Blindly rebalancing on a fixed calendar, without considering context, can be just as destructive. If your portfolio contains high-conviction positions or thematic tilts, arbitrary rebalancing may blunt your edge. On the other hand, *never rebalancing leads to drift*—your intended risk profile quietly morphs into something else. A 60/40 portfolio can become an 80/20 one without any intentional decision, simply because equities outperformed over time.

The deeper skill is learning *when* to rebalance—and more importantly, when not to. This requires a blend of structural logic and philosophical self-knowledge. Structural logic means having defined allocation bands or tolerances: for example, a rule that if an asset class drifts more than 5% from its target weight, it triggers review. This prevents you from acting reactively and creates a behavioural circuit breaker. But *philosophical self-knowledge is the more subtle layer.* It means understanding what your portfolio is *for*—what beliefs it represents, what risks you are willing to hold, and what role each asset plays.

Imagine a portfolio with a 30% allocation to global equities, 20% to emerging markets, 25% to fixed income, 15% to real assets, and 10% in experimental or thematic positions. Now imagine emerging markets fall 25% over three months. Does that justify trimming them further? Or does it warrant adding? Without a predefined answer, most investors guess. But a values-based approach starts from a different question: *"Has anything changed about my core thesis for this exposure?"* If not, you may view the drawdown as an opportunity to restore balance. If the thesis has eroded, you review—not based on performance, but on validity.

The most seasoned investors often view rebalancing as a discipline of honouring the original blueprint—not as an excuse for tinkering. They know that market noise will always tempt them to intervene, but true discipline lies in resisting the urge to act unless a meaningful threshold is met. This is why many institutional investors use *trigger-based rebalancing frameworks*: they rebalance only when drift exceeds a statistically meaningful band, not based on calendar intervals or headlines.

There is also a distinction between *systemic rebalancing* and *tactical repositioning*. The former is rule-based, designed to maintain the portfolio's intended shape. The latter is discretionary, based on short-term views or perceived mispricings. Too often, investors confuse the two. They sell an outperforming sector not to restore balance, but because they fear it has peaked. Or they avoid adding to a fallen position because it feels risky—even if it fits the system. *This is where panic creeps in disguised as prudence.*

To avoid this confusion, one powerful tool is the *rebalance log*. Before executing any rebalance, write down: What asset am I adjusting? What is its target vs actual weight? What has changed? Is this a system-driven rebalance or a belief-driven adjustment? What signal am I using? This log creates friction—not to slow you down unnecessarily, but to ensure your action is driven by structure, not sentiment.

Let's look at a practical example. During the COVID-19 market crash in March 2020, many investors abandoned equities, going to cash or defensive positions. Others who had pre-set rebalancing rules found themselves *buying into the dip*, restoring equity weightings that had been crushed by the selloff. In the months that followed, those who had bought when it felt uncomfortable were rewarded handsomely. This wasn't prescience—it was adherence. Their rebalancing system gave them a reason to act against emotion, and they had the courage to trust it.

But the goal is not to win every quarter. The purpose of disciplined rebalancing is to *sustain alignment* with your strategy over decades. If you allow recency bias to dominate—overweighting recent winners, avoiding recent losers—you are not investing, you are following momentum in disguise. A values-led portfolio rebalance says: "This is how much I believe in this asset. This is the role it plays. Unless my beliefs or goals have changed, I will honour its place."

There is also a psychological benefit. Rebalancing, done thoughtfully, reinforces identity. Each action says something about who you are as an investor. Are you a trend chaser? A long-term allocator? A thematic believer? The act of trimming a soaring position—even when it feels thrilling—can be a moral commitment to humility. The act of adding to a hated asset—even when it feels contrarian—can be a testament to your discipline. *Each rebalance is a behavioural imprint that shapes your investment character.*

Still, no system is perfect. There will be moments when your values and the market diverge. You may believe in clean energy, but the sector underperforms for years. You may trust global diversification, but home-market bias keeps outperforming. In these moments, rebalancing becomes an existential decision: *Am I willing to keep reflecting my values, even when they are out of favour?* This is where conviction and resilience intersect. Not rebalancing blindly—but also not abandoning principles too quickly.

Ultimately, the question is not just when to rebalance, but *why*. Is the change being made because your investment thesis evolved? Because a risk exposure is now out of proportion to your tolerance? Or simply because the market made you feel nervous? Clarity here is everything. Panic is a symptom of poor process. But when you use rebalancing as a *ritual of alignment*, not a reaction to discomfort, it becomes one of the most powerful tools in your arsenal.

Your portfolio does not require constant pruning. But it does require intentional upkeep. Like a well-built structure, it can withstand stress if the foundation is sound and the maintenance is principled. Rebalancing is not about constantly tweaking the design. It's about checking whether the structure still reflects what you set out to build—and having the composure to restore that structure when the winds of the market blow it off course. The key is to act from values, not vibes. And when that distinction becomes a habit, your portfolio begins to carry the signature of someone who knows what they believe—and invests like it.

Chapter 8
Thinking in Decades, Acting in Moments

Every investor quietly manages two portfolios. One is tangible: a collection of holdings, weights, and returns visible on a brokerage screen. The other is intangible, residing in the mind: a mix of ambitions, anxieties, nascent strategies, and personal narratives. Over time, it becomes clear that success with the first is inseparable from mastery of the second. Compounding is not confined to capital; it applies equally to behaviour, discipline, learning, and identity. The most enduring returns rest upon psychological infrastructure.

This chapter is not about forecasting the next decade. It is about navigating ten years of investing without being hijacked by ten seconds of impulse. Temporal agility—the capacity to maintain a long-range vision while acting in the immediacy of markets—is arguably the most underrated skill in finance. Too often, people act on emotion and later rationalise with long-term justification. The inverse—making daily decisions that faithfully serve a much broader vision—requires deliberate thought and structure.

Yet clarity of vision is rare. Ask someone about their retirement plan, and you will hear vague numbers; about risk tolerance, and you hear generalities; about long-term financial philosophy, and you may encounter silence. Many investors have not defined the person they aspire to become—they know they should invest and wish to grow wealth, but they lack a guiding north star. Without one, external noise will fill the void: market swings, social media, pundit opinions, macroeconomic chatter. These forces are loud, persuasive, and rarely aligned with personal values.

The most strategic investors begin not with a stock, but with a temporal framework. Success is defined not by quarterly outperformance, but by becoming the kind of investor whose process compounds reliably across cycles. One effective tool is the future-self letter: a written message from the investor you aim to be ten years hence, addressed to your present self. Far from whimsical, it serves as a behavioural anchor. By articulating your ideal temperament, habits, and decision-making principles, you create a reference point that endures beyond models, predictions, or fleeting market commentary.

Consider a letter beginning: "I no longer check prices daily. I trust the structure I've built. I review annually, study quarterly. I rebalance according to values, not nervousness. I follow businesses, not narratives. I hold through noise and adjust with intention. Thank you for starting." These are operational instructions, drafted in calm reflection, meant to guide you in moments of market turbulence.

This philosophy extends naturally to using a calendar as a control mechanism. Most investors react to the market's rhythm: volatility prompts action, quiet periods induce drift. Savvy investors invert this. They impose fixed schedules for portfolio reviews, strategy sessions, and study days. Quarterly audits, annual reflections, monthly research—these temporal guardrails shape behaviour, prevent overreaction, and redirect focus from short-term noise to deliberate planning. They prompt vital questions: Has my thesis changed? Has risk exposure drifted? Have I encountered new information that challenges prior beliefs? Without such rituals, one defaults to the emotional cadence of screens and headlines.

Learning is integral to the portfolio itself. Intellectual humility, though often celebrated in theory, must be embedded in practice. Knowledge compounds like capital; allocate time and effort accordingly. Set goals not merely for returns but for readings completed, theses re-evaluated, and biases interrogated. Track insights as you would earnings. Journals become a ledger of thought, auditing reasoning rather than prices.

Resilient thought demands multidisciplinarity. Charlie Munger has long championed this, but it must be operationalised: study history, psychology, biology, engineering. Examine how systems evolve, how incentives warp judgement, how failures propagate. These are not tangential exercises—they are foundational for decision-making when narratives shift rapidly. The ability to process complexity outside finance is an unpriced advantage.

Finally, exit strategy must be reframed. It is not a signal of panic, nor an admission of failure, but an articulation of values. To define when and why you will exit is to assert control over risk, not succumb to emotion. Exit decisions should be value-triggered, not event-triggered: if the underlying rationale no longer holds, if a company's cash-flow model collapses, or if the asset no longer fits the portfolio's risk-return framework, then action is warranted. This transforms selling from a reactive impulse into a deliberate, principle-driven act.

This chapter is not about robotic execution. It is about deliberate design. Thinking in decades is not a denial of the present; it is a reinterpretation of it. Every market action reflects a worldview: are you reinforcing the investor you aim to become, or responding to external pressures? Long-term thinking is a muscle strengthened by systems, structure, and self-honesty.

As you progress, you will be asked to examine your decision cadence, intellectual intake, and behavioural architecture. You will be guided to envision your future self and reverse-engineer the systems that lead there—not through sheer will, but through alignment and design. Thinking in decades while acting in moments requires more than patience; it demands an identity that withstands volatility, outlasts trends, and reflects values consistently. That is the true edge—and it is established long before a single trade is made.

Imagining Your 10-Year Future as an Investor:

Most people overestimate what they can do in a year and underestimate what they can accomplish in a decade. Nowhere is this more evident than in investing. The allure of short-term gains, quick wins, or avoiding losses tends to dominate our thinking, while the quiet compounding of long-term discipline is underestimated, even dismissed. But the most consistently successful investors aren't the ones who obsess over timing the next move—they are the ones who build toward a clear, coherent identity as investors. That identity is not something you find. It's something you design.

A powerful and underused tool in this process is writing a letter to yourself from the vantage point of ten years in the future. This is not motivational fluff. It is an exercise in strategic imagination. When done properly, it forces you to translate vague intentions into tangible outcomes. It gives structure to the abstract, rigour to your aspirations, and clarity to what matters most. In a world of endless noise, *this is a filtering mechanism for your attention.*

The investor you want to become already exists—just not yet. They're shaped by thousands of small decisions you'll make between now and then. Decisions about when to act, when to wait, what to study, how to respond to losses, and what you believe about risk, reward, and responsibility. Left unexamined, these decisions drift. They conform to headlines, to social media sentiment, to whichever guru has the loudest voice that month. But when anchored to a clear future identity, they cohere into something purposeful.

Begin by imagining the most grounded version of yourself as an investor a decade from now. What habits have become second nature? What behaviours have you outgrown? What types of companies or assets do you understand deeply and hold with conviction? How do you approach volatility—not theoretically, but practically? What does your portfolio reflect—not just financially, but philosophically? And, most tellingly, what have you stopped doing?

Now write. Address the letter from that future self to your current self. Make it specific. Detail your process, your values, your routines, your blind spots. Describe how you allocate attention, not just capital. Talk about what you've learned—not from reading, but from doing. Include the mistakes you're proud of making early, because they taught you what matters. Include the principles you refused to compromise on, even when markets tempted you. *This letter is not an aspiration; it is an operating manual.*

The practice draws from a well-established concept in behavioural psychology: future-self continuity. Studies have shown that people who feel emotionally connected to their future selves are more likely to delay gratification, make healthier decisions, and act with integrity under uncertainty. When you craft a vivid, specific, and internally consistent image of your future investor identity, you become more likely to align your present behaviour with that version of yourself. The exercise isn't wishful thinking—it's behavioural engineering.

This shift also changes how you measure progress. Most investors default to benchmarks: the S&P 500, their peers, even a past version of themselves. But a letter from your future self gives you an internal benchmark. You start to ask better questions. Did this quarter's decision reflect the investor I'm trying to become? Did I respond to volatility the way I said I would? Did I take time to review, reflect, and recalibrate? Or did I get swept up in the moment, again?

This recalibration is especially critical during market downturns. In those moments, the emotional intensity of loss can eclipse long-term logic. Fear whispers in your ear that the market is broken, that your strategy is flawed, that maybe you're just not cut out for this. Having your own words—written during a period of clarity—act as a counterbalance. They remind you of the logic, not the mood, that should govern your next move. *The letter becomes an internal circuit-breaker for panic.*

Consider an example: a young investor named Asha begins her investing journey with a deep fear of volatility. She reads widely, builds a diversified portfolio, and performs well for two years. Then a sudden downturn wipes out 20% of her portfolio. She panics. But then she returns to the letter she wrote to herself at the outset. It reads, "When the market corrects—and it will—you will want to sell. You will feel foolish. You'll start doubting your thesis. But you built this portfolio knowing this day would come. You don't need to act. You need to observe. Let this moment be a teacher." That one paragraph saves her from a costly error. Not because she was reminded what to do, but because she was reminded *who she wanted to be.*

The letter-writing exercise also reveals latent contradictions. Perhaps you say you want to be a patient investor but constantly chase speculative growth stocks. Or you say you value simplicity but hold 45 positions with no thematic coherence. These inconsistencies are hard to detect in real time. But when you define the identity you're aiming for, they become harder to justify. You start pruning not just your portfolio, but your behaviours.

This exercise is not static. It can be revisited annually—refined as you gain experience, insight, and context. You might adjust your goals, sharpen your convictions, or rewrite assumptions that didn't hold up. That's not weakness; it's evolution. The point is not to lock yourself into a rigid identity. It is to ensure that your investing decisions are tethered to *something internally defined*, not externally imposed.

Importantly, this practice also inoculates you against performance obsession. You stop chasing perfect entry points or flawless returns because you realise your real advantage is not timing—it's time. Your focus shifts from prediction to process, from control to clarity. Over time, this mindset frees you from the tyranny of perfectionism and the illusion of constant optimisation. You become less concerned with looking smart and more committed to becoming wise.

There's also a cultural undercurrent here. In a world saturated with noise, performance porn, and algorithm-driven dopamine hits, writing a letter to your future self is a deeply subversive act. It requires slowness, thoughtfulness, and emotional courage. It insists on reflection in a world that worships reaction. Most of all, it restores agency. Because the future of your portfolio is not dictated by markets alone. It is shaped—quietly and powerfully—by your beliefs, your behaviour, and your ability to define both.

To invest without a sense of your future self is to walk through fog with a broken compass. To invest *with* that sense is to move through uncertainty with a kind of internal certainty—not that outcomes will always go your way, but that your process, anchored in self-awareness, will outlast temporary turbulence.

So write the letter. Make it real. Make it awkward, imperfect, honest. Store it where you can find it when you're tempted to deviate. Let it age with you. Let it reveal how far you've come and how far you still have to go. Because the most successful investors are not those who guessed best. They are those who grew best. And that growth begins not with a trade, but with a conversation—with the investor you've not yet become, but still can.

The Calendar as a Behavioural Tool:

Most investors overestimate what they need to know and underestimate what they need to practise. Information is abundant; discipline is rare. And in no domain is that more evident than in the calendar—the ordinary tool almost no one uses to its fullest. In investing, time is your strongest ally, but only if you build a structure that invites it into your decision-making. The most consistently effective investors don't just track markets. They *schedule reflection, review, and recalibration with the same seriousness as capital allocation.*

The calendar, when used well, becomes far more than a place to record dividend dates or tax deadlines. It becomes a behavioural framework—a system for designing your own attention. Left unguided, your attention is hijacked by whatever is loudest, most recent, or emotionally provocative. Headlines, analyst predictions, or social media noise become proxies for strategy. But when you embed checkpoints into your year, your attention becomes intentional. You're no longer reacting. You're observing, assessing, and adapting on your own terms.

Imagine two investors with identical portfolios. One checks their holdings impulsively, driven by mood or market movements. The other follows a calendar-based rhythm—monthly reviews, quarterly check-ins, and annual strategic overhauls. After five years, their results diverge. Not because one has superior information, but because *one has a process that protects against behavioural erosion.*

The question is not whether you should use a calendar. The question is how thoughtfully you've designed it. What belongs on your investing calendar is not merely transactional. It must include space for reflection, learning, and strategic realignment. A quarterly earnings date might belong on the same calendar as a biannual check-in with your long-term goals. A monthly snapshot of portfolio drift might appear alongside a reminder to revisit an investment thesis. It's not about becoming robotic. It's about becoming deliberate.

Begin with the annual structure. At least once a year, block a dedicated session to step outside the spreadsheet. This is your strategic review—not to react to market performance, but to evaluate your portfolio's alignment with your beliefs, objectives, and current context. Ask: *Has anything changed in my worldview? Has my tolerance for risk evolved? Do I still understand and believe in the core positions I hold?* Avoid performance obsession during this session. The real question isn't "Did I beat the market?" It's "Did I follow my process, and is it still sound?"

Then move to the quarterly rhythm. This is the ideal cadence for operational adjustments—evaluating diversification, reviewing thesis drift, and checking whether any holdings are no longer intellectually or emotionally defensible. It is also the right interval to ask whether your current allocation still reflects your highest-conviction ideas. Do not confuse action with improvement. Sometimes the best adjustment is restraint. *The goal is not to make changes. It is to give yourself structured permission to consider them.*

Monthly checkpoints, by contrast, should be lightweight. They are not for trading decisions but for behavioural audits. Did you panic during volatility? Did you follow the rules you set for yourself? Did you consume more market news than was useful? These quick reviews help build a feedback loop between your intentions and your behaviours. Over time, these small reflections compound into stronger discipline. They also expose patterns: the temptation to tinker after reading a newsletter, or the tendency to sell during market dips. Knowing these tendencies gives you leverage over them.

Finally, incorporate learning into your calendar—not passively, but with intent. Allocate time each month or quarter to deepen your understanding of a sector, revisit a classic investing text, or review a mistake in your portfolio. Create a space in your schedule for study, not just for scanning. This transforms learning from a vague aspiration into a tracked behaviour. It also prevents knowledge from becoming disconnected from decision-making. *A calendar entry for reading is a commitment to sharpening your thinking, not just broadening your exposure.*

What sets calendar-based investors apart is not rigid discipline but thoughtful iteration. You are not creating a mechanical process for the sake of control. You are designing *a rhythm that matches the tempo of your goals.* Fast goals need faster loops. Long-term goals require wide-angle lenses. Most investors use the wrong lens at the wrong time. They zoom in daily on long-term holdings and zoom out annually on short-term impulses. A calendar corrects this mismatch by assigning the right time horizon to the right decision.

Crucially, your calendar also acts as a defence against overreaction. During moments of market mania or panic, the temptation to act is overwhelming. But if you've pre-committed to act only during your scheduled reviews, you give yourself breathing room. You buy time to think instead of time to *feel.* Investors who make changes in real-time tend to overfit their strategy to current events. Investors who follow a schedule make decisions in context, not in crisis.

There is a parallel here with physical health. No elite athlete trains based on how they feel in the moment. They follow cycles: build, rest, test, recover. They don't lift heavier every day. They adapt their programme based on structured feedback. The calendar becomes a system for sustainable growth. Investing is no different. If every market dip feels like a reason to act, or every rally feels like a missed opportunity, you are not investing—you are reacting. The calendar introduces structure into chaos.

Consider a practical case. Rahul, a self-directed investor with a demanding career, used to check his portfolio several times a day. He often made impulsive changes—tweaking allocation, selling on fear, chasing recent winners. His returns were inconsistent, and worse, he felt emotionally drained. Then he implemented a structured calendar: monthly behavioural check-ins, quarterly portfolio reviews, and a yearly strategy update. The number of trades he made dropped by 70%. His satisfaction increased. His performance stabilised. But the biggest shift was psychological—*he felt in control without being controlling.*

It's easy to dismiss a calendar as too simple to matter. But simplicity is not the same as superficiality. In fact, most investors fail not because they lacked information, but because they lacked rhythm. When everything is urgent, nothing is important. When you embed your process into time itself, you transform your calendar from a container of appointments into *a compass for integrity.*

To invest well over time, you must learn to manage not just money but attention, energy, and intention. The calendar allows you to do exactly that. It is not about micromanaging every move, but about shaping a cadence that protects against drift, distraction, and delusion. The best investors are not those who stare hardest at the screen. They are those who *build thinking into time*, and revisit their decisions at the pace of clarity—not emotion.

Your portfolio lives on spreadsheets. But your behaviour lives on calendars. Align the two, and you stop guessing your way through the year. You start thinking like someone whose process, not just whose picks, will stand the test of decades.

Learning as a Portfolio Asset:

The most underleveraged asset in any investor's toolkit isn't a strategy, fund, or signal—it's intellectual growth. Capital compounds, but so does comprehension. While financial markets reward patience and discipline, they ultimately punish stagnation of thought. If your thinking is not evolving, your edge is quietly eroding. The investor who treats learning as a cost rather than a compounding asset will eventually find their portfolio misaligned with both the world and themselves.

Investing is not static. Markets shift, companies transform, technology redefines industries, and behavioural dynamics respond to evolving narratives. If your mental models are relics of a previous cycle, your decisions are built on sediment, not structure. What's needed is not relentless reaction to new headlines, but *intentional learning designed to sharpen discernment.* Investing well over decades means committing to a lifelong apprenticeship in judgement.

The myth that investors are born with talent is seductive, but ultimately lazy. Great investors are not clairvoyant—they are intellectually athletic. They revisit ideas, challenge assumptions, and revise their mental playbooks without pride or panic. They develop structured ways of learning—curated reading habits, reflective practices, and intellectual routines that feed insight rather than inflate confidence. *They are as committed to learning as they are to returns.*

Yet most individual investors spend more time refreshing a stock chart than studying its underlying drivers. They track prices obsessively and principles rarely. Worse, they equate learning with following financial influencers, mistaking volume for value. But passive consumption is not the same as active understanding. Reading ten articles doesn't equal clarity if the ideas are shallow, contradictory, or unchecked. *To learn in a way that improves your investing, you must treat information as nutrition, not entertainment.*

One powerful shift is to treat learning as an intentional line item in your investing life—not an afterthought, but an asset class of its own. Imagine allocating not just capital, but time: one hour each week for reading, one hour each month for reflection, and one longer session each quarter for strategic review. This rhythm, once embedded, becomes a flywheel. Ideas build on each other. Concepts mature. You revisit your own beliefs with more depth, less ego.

A compelling case study comes from the letters of Howard Marks, co-founder of Oaktree Capital. His memos are not forecasts. They are frameworks—distilled reflections shaped by decades of reading, observing, and synthesising. They serve as both a chronicle of market behaviour and a model of intellectual discipline. The reason Marks is widely respected is not merely his returns—it is the rigour of his thinking. He writes to think, and he reads to sharpen the lens through which he sees value.

For individual investors, the takeaway is profound: *thinking must become a tracked practice.* This means more than just reading broadly. It requires learning with filters, asking: "What am I trying to understand? What type of information challenges or refines my current convictions?" Set clear learning goals, much as you would for saving or asset allocation. Target reading a certain number of annual letters, sector primers, or history-rich analyses. Track not just what you read, but what changed because of it.

Reflection is the second pillar of intellectual compounding. Without it, learning is inert. Many investors absorb facts but rarely examine their decisions. They skip over losses, deny the role of luck, and attribute gains to skill. This leads to a fragile intellect—one that survives only when the wind is at its back. To counteract this, create a personal review system. After each investment decision—win or loss—write a debrief: What did I believe? What was my evidence? What would I do differently now? *This isn't a diary of regret—it's a journal of progression.*

Some of the best institutional investors treat investment memos not as compliance documents, but as tools for future insight. They don't just justify a purchase; they log their reasoning to revisit it later. When performance diverges from expectations, they don't ask, "What went wrong?" They ask, "Where was the original thinking flawed—or too shallow?" This kind of iterative honesty is what separates those who learn from those who merely remember.

Importantly, learning should also include historical fluency. Many of the worst decisions in investing are born of historical ignorance—believing that "this time is different," or that valuation doesn't matter, or that exponential narratives will never collapse. Yet the study of market history—whether through books like *Manias, Panics, and Crashes* or through post-mortems of fund blowups—is the best antidote to narrative intoxication. *Learning history is not about avoiding mistakes others made. It's about understanding how and why those mistakes felt rational at the time.*

Another overlooked source of intellectual return is cross-disciplinary reading. The investor who reads only finance becomes myopic. The one who reads broadly—psychology, history, biology, statistics—builds a toolkit of mental models that work across contexts. Charlie Munger called this a latticework of understanding. It's what allows great investors to assess not just balance sheets, but human behaviour, probability, and systems thinking. *You are not trying to memorise formulas. You are trying to upgrade your filters for reality.*

This is not to suggest that learning should become a fetish of its own. There is such a thing as overconsumption, especially when it replaces action. But the point is to establish a rhythm where learning is proactive, cumulative, and directional. When learning becomes a background process, rather than a foreground commitment, you plateau. When it becomes ritualised—scheduled, tracked, and reviewed—it becomes an engine.

Consider another analogy: learning as maintenance. Just as a car requires oil changes, your thinking requires tune-ups. Just as a plane undergoes pre-flight checks, your portfolio decisions should pass through a checklist of intellectual rigour. And just as elite athletes study film between games, serious investors revisit and refine their thought processes between decisions. *Learning, then, is not decorative. It is operational.*

Over time, the compounding effect of intellectual investment begins to show. Your decisions become faster, not because you are guessing, but because you are recognising. Your confidence becomes quieter, because it is grounded. You need less external validation, because you trust your internal clarity. And most importantly, you begin to see investing not as a contest of prediction, but as a craft of understanding.

None of this happens automatically. You must choose to build a learning architecture. That may mean creating a reading stack, a note-taking system, or a learning partner to discuss ideas with. It may mean setting annual learning goals, just as you set financial ones. It may mean spending less time on fast opinions and more time on slow insights. Whatever the mechanism, the mindset is the same: *treat learning not as preparation for investing, but as part of the investing itself.*

At a certain level of experience, all investors face diminishing returns from new information. But no one faces diminishing returns from refined understanding. The more you learn, the more you can unlearn what no longer serves. The sharper your models, the less you are swayed by noise. In this way, learning becomes not just an asset—it becomes a filter, a buffer, and a compass.

Investors who think only in terms of markets rarely outperform those who also think in terms of ideas. Over decades, it is not the strategy alone that drives returns—it is the mind behind it. And minds, like portfolios, must be tended, tracked, and nurtured.

If you believe that your money should work for you, then believe this also: your mind must grow with it. Learning is not optional. It is leverage. The question is not whether you have the time to learn. The question is whether you have the discipline to turn learning into a process—one that outlasts bull runs, outthinks volatility, and outperforms inertia.

Exit Strategy as an Expression of Values:

Most investors obsess over when to buy. Far fewer give equal weight to the act of exiting—yet it's this final decision that often defines the integrity of the entire process. Exits are not just technical events. They are emotional thresholds, moral checkpoints, and philosophical expressions of who you are as an investor. If your entries reflect your aspirations, your exits reveal your maturity.

An exit is not failure. Nor is it surrender. It is simply the disciplined end to a decision cycle. Yet many investors delay exits until pain forces their hand, or euphoria convinces them they're invincible. This reactive mindset is not just suboptimal—it's dangerous. *The absence of a clear exit strategy turns every investment into an open-ended emotional liability*. Whether the trigger is panic during a drawdown or greed during a rally, lack of pre-commitment to exit criteria hands your portfolio over to your most unreliable decision-maker: your mood.

To exit well, you must begin with clarity—not about price targets or technical patterns, but about personal values. Why did you invest in this asset to begin with? What role does it serve in your portfolio? What would have to change—about the asset, or about your thesis—for you to exit with integrity? These are not questions to ask *after* things go wrong. They are questions that form the backbone of responsible ownership. *Your exit plan is not a market call; it is a mirror of your convictions, constraints, and intentions.*

Consider the investor who buys into a high-growth tech stock because they believe in its long-term disruption story. If that conviction is genuine, they should be prepared to weather earnings misses, analyst downgrades, or even sector rotations—*as long as the underlying thesis remains intact.* But if their real motive was short-term momentum or fear of missing out, then they're more likely to sell at the first sign of weakness, not because the thesis broke, but because their emotional threshold was shallow. *Without a values-based exit plan, conviction masquerades as convenience.*

The most effective investors document their exit conditions in advance. Not just the obvious, like "if it drops 30%," but also qualitative shifts: "if the CEO changes and the company pivots strategy," or "if the valuation detaches permanently from fundamentals." This forces clarity of purpose. It reduces ambiguity during chaos. And it separates regret from reflection when exits eventually happen. Because they *will* happen—either by your decision or the market's.

Take institutional investors. The best fund managers maintain internal frameworks that define when to trim, when to liquidate, and when to hold despite turbulence. These frameworks are rarely rigid algorithms. They are adaptive but anchored—guided by a pre-agreed investment philosophy and risk tolerance. *Their strength lies not in prediction, but in pre-commitment.* They rehearse exit scenarios before they are emotionally hijacked by them. Individual investors should learn from this discipline, not dismiss it as inaccessible.

There's also an ethical dimension to exits. If you own a company whose practices violate your values—say, in environmental impact or governance—you must consider whether continuing to hold it is an implicit endorsement. Many investors outsource this decision to ESG filters or indexes, but doing so risks moral passivity. A personal exit framework asks you to define, in your own terms, *what kinds of businesses you are willing to profit from—and when you are no longer comfortable doing so.* In this way, exits become an expression of responsibility, not just strategy.

Another case worth examining is the exit amid euphoric gains. Investors often struggle more with selling winners than cutting losers. They fear missing out on further upside or disrupting a winning streak. Yet *failing to define an exit can lead to round-tripping gains—that is, watching an asset rise and fall back without ever taking profits.* Here, a values-based framework asks: "What is enough?" At what point does continuing to hold a rapidly appreciating asset no longer align with your financial needs or risk appetite?

A well-defined exit strategy also protects against the tyranny of sunk cost. It enables you to treat each decision with fresh eyes, rather than clinging to a position out of pride, nostalgia, or the irrational desire to 'get back to even'. Investors who fail to exit losing positions often rationalise their inertia with flawed logic—"It's already down so much, I might as well wait." But *exit discipline requires a different lens: if I didn't already own this, would I buy it today at this price with this thesis?* If the answer is no, you're not holding a position—you're holding a wound.

This logic applies equally to rebalancing. Sometimes an exit is not a full liquidation, but a trim—reducing exposure after outperformance to maintain balance with your broader goals. Rebalancing is often framed as a mechanical act, but it, too, reflects values. It says: "I'm not chasing the hottest trend; I'm honouring my long-term allocation." It says: "I trust my process more than my impulses." *Exits grounded in values allow you to adjust without drifting.*

There is also the question of timing exits around life changes. For example, approaching retirement may warrant strategic de-risking—not because the market is signalling danger, but because *your life is demanding predictability.* A thoughtful exit strategy should not only reflect market dynamics, but also *personal seasonality*: job transitions, family responsibilities, or shifts in liquidity needs. The best portfolios are built not just for performance, but for relevance. Exits, then, become tools of alignment.

Of course, no exit strategy can eliminate all regret. You will sometimes sell too early. You will sometimes hold too long. But the goal is not perfection. The goal is *coherence.* An exit plan that reflects your values, risk appetite, and strategic framework allows you to evaluate outcomes with clarity, not shame. You don't need to get every exit right. You need to make them *for the right reasons.*

One practical recommendation is to include an "Exit Intent" section in your investment notes—just a few sentences that articulate your conditions for reassessment. Not a fixed sell price, but a scenario map. This could include factors like valuation thresholds, competitive changes, macro shifts, or personal priorities. Revisit this note quarterly. Use it as a sober reference point when volatility tests your resolve.

The broader point is this: *your exits reveal what you truly believe about risk, control, and purpose.* If you let markets decide for you, you forfeit agency. If you let fear or greed hijack your timing, you sacrifice returns to emotion. But if you design exits with intention, you regain ownership of the process. Not because you'll always exit at the top—but because you'll always exit on terms you can respect.

Exits should be treated with the same philosophical depth as entries. They are not just about capital preservation—they are about psychological stewardship. Every sale is a vote of confidence in your own process, a closing of one chapter so you can allocate attention and energy to the next. In this sense, a good exit is not reactive. It is generative. It clears the path for better decisions, sharper thinking, and deeper conviction.

So do not delay crafting your own exit framework until you are under pressure. Do it now, while calm, curious, and rational. Ask: What would it take for me to sell this asset? What would change in my life or in the world that would require a different approach? What do I want to avoid repeating from past exit mistakes? These are not abstract questions. They are design principles for investing with integrity.

You will exit every position eventually. The only question is whether that exit will be thoughtful or reflexive, aligned or arbitrary. Build a system now that ensures your exits reflect your values, not your anxieties. Because in the end, how you leave the trade says more about you than how you entered it.

Chapter 9
Investing as Self-Knowledge

Few experiences expose our inner workings as directly as investing. On the surface, it presents numbers, charts, and ratios—but beneath that veneer lies a far more revealing arena: how we confront uncertainty, measure progress, and grapple with control, patience, and purpose. Markets do more than test technical skill; they hold up a mirror to temperament, priorities, and mental architecture. If you pay attention, investing becomes a tool of self-inquiry as much as a financial exercise.

This chapter does not dwell on asset allocation or economic theory. It explores introspection through action—learning who you are by observing your behaviour when real money is at stake. Risk tolerance, often treated as a checkbox on a brokerage form, is far more nuanced. It evolves with context and reflects your personal narrative: formative experiences, cultural background, ambitions, and anxieties. It reveals itself most sharply when markets fall 20 per cent and you must decide whether to sell, hold, or add.

Time preference—the capacity to delay gratification—shapes your approach to capital allocation in equally profound ways. Can you hold an investment for five, ten years without interference, or are you compelled to check prices repeatedly, seeking reassurance? These behaviours are far from trivial; they echo across careers, relationships, and other spheres demanding focus. Every trade carries an emotional signature.

Understanding yourself as an investor is not optional; it is central to strategy. Without it, one is vulnerable to comparison, hype cycles, and mimetic behaviour, abandoning long-term plans when benchmarks underperform. Self-knowledge anchors decisions in personal context rather than in the shifting priorities of the crowd.

Investing should be treated as a living reflection of evolving values. Periodic reflection is as crucial as financial review. Ask yourself: why am I investing? What life am I funding with this capital? Which trade-offs am I willing to accept, and which am I not? These questions inform decisions about asset mix, risk exposure, time horizon, and the volatility you can genuinely tolerate.

The chapter also interrogates the pitfalls of value-signalling under the banner of ethical investing. ESG has become a buzzword-laden arena, but the real question is whether your allocations reflect your values or merely chase returns. More importantly, are those values truly examined, or borrowed from slogans and marketing materials? Authentic investing demands direct engagement with what matters to you—be it sustainability, justice, innovation, or intergenerational continuity.

Legacy, too, is considered—not narrowly as inheritance, but as stewardship. Even first-time investors shape the future through capital allocation. These futures are philosophical as well as financial: what principles will outlive account balances? Will your heirs inherit a spreadsheet, or a framework for reasoning? A portfolio, or a worldview? Thinking in terms of legacy extends the horizon, reframing money as a resource for intentionality and encouraging systems that outlast transient moods.

Defining "enough" is critical. Left vague, it becomes a moving target, driven by social comparison or unconscious ambition. Clear boundaries prevent both overaccumulation and premature liquidation. When "enough" is understood, discipline comes naturally; investing becomes aligned with life goals rather than reactionary impulses. Every decision—from asset selection to philanthropy—becomes sharper, guided by clarity rather than compulsion.

Throughout, the chapter examines the layers of self revealed through investing: the impulsive self seeking action, the fearful self avoiding loss, the aspirational self imagining greatness, and the reflective self quietly observing. Suppression is unnecessary; recognition is essential. Self-knowledge means identifying which voice drives you in any moment and choosing which to heed.

Practical tools—journaling frameworks, reflection prompts, goal-setting exercises—are presented not as productivity hacks but as mirrors, helping you witness patterns, evolve behaviour, and cultivate awareness. Perfection is not required; presence is. Without it, the market writes your narrative for you.

Ultimately, investing shapes character as much as capital. Superficial measures—returns, rankings, metrics—offer comfort but little insight. True success lies in resilience under pressure, alignment with values, and steadiness amid chaos. Growth is not abandoned; it is grounded in ethics, self-awareness, and long-term purpose. When strategies falter and circumstances shift—as they inevitably do—the only reliable compass is the investor's self.

You need not adopt asceticism to invest with depth. Honesty suffices. The process will reveal priorities, blind spots, beliefs, and pretense. Those willing to study themselves as rigorously as they study stocks discover that wealth accrues alongside character. And that, in the end, is a return worth pursuing.

How Investing Reveals (and Shapes) Your Identity:

Every financial decision contains a fingerprint. Embedded in each trade, allocation, or hesitation is a deeper signal—how you process uncertainty, what you believe about control, how you respond to pressure, and what you ultimately value. Most investors assume they are merely applying logic to markets. But markets don't just react to reason—they respond to emotion, narrative, and belief. Which is why the process of investing, if approached with awareness, can act as a powerful diagnostic. *Your behaviour around money reveals more about you than you might be ready to admit.*

Let's begin with risk tolerance—not as a numerical category assigned by an onboarding questionnaire, but as a lived reality. It's easy to say you're "comfortable with volatility" when the market is rising. But the real test surfaces in moments of drawdown. When prices fall 20%, do you feel curious or panicked? Do you view dips as opportunities, or do you interpret them as signals of personal failure or market collapse? The answer is rarely about finance alone. It's shaped by your history—how money was discussed (or not) in your childhood, whether you've experienced job loss or instability, how you perceive control, and how you internalise loss.

Risk tolerance isn't fixed. It evolves with your context, your resources, and your mindset. But what matters most is that you *observe it honestly*. Too many investors build portfolios based on who they want to be—not who they are. They mimic bold strategies, embrace leverage, or chase volatile assets without first asking: *Can I live with the consequences of this decision?* Not in theory. In practice. In a market crash. In a job transition. In a health crisis. Risk, properly understood, is personal. It is not what the market does—it is what the market's movements *do to you.*

This brings us to time preference—the degree to which you are willing to delay gratification. Economists tend to treat time preference as a rational input. But in the real world, it is *psychologically revealing*. Do you have the patience to let compounding do its work? Or do you crave the dopamine of short-term wins? This tension shows up in your asset selection (index funds vs. options trading), your time horizon (years vs. weeks), and your reaction to headlines (measured rebalancing vs. impulsive sell-offs). High time preference often correlates with distraction, over-trading, and goal drift. Low time preference, on the other hand, tends to be rooted in clarity, self-trust, and broader life alignment. *The more you can zoom out, the less you are hostage to noise.*

Your reaction to stress may be the most honest signal of all. No spreadsheet can prepare you for the emotional weight of watching a portfolio lose five or six figures in value. In such moments, you meet yourself. Are you the kind of person who doubles down, freezes, seeks reassurance, or lashes out? Do you start obsessively reading financial news or avoid logging in to your account altogether? Do you catastrophise, imagining worst-case scenarios, or can you hold your frame and evaluate probabilities? *Your stress response during market volatility is a reflection of your broader emotional regulation system.*

Stress exposure doesn't automatically make you wiser. But if you *study* how you respond, it can. The key is to treat market stress as data, not diagnosis. If you sell during a panic, it doesn't mean you're a "bad" investor—it means you've uncovered a point of friction between your plan and your psychology. That insight is gold. It tells you where your next layer of growth lies—not just as an investor, but as a thinker. Self-observation is the bridge between volatility and wisdom.

There's also a subtler identity dynamic at play in investing: *status awareness*. Do you find yourself comparing your returns to others? Are you quietly chasing alpha to prove something—not just to the market, but to peers, family, or an imagined audience? Many people anchor their investment strategies not in objective analysis, but in *social proximity*. If everyone in your circle is talking about tech stocks, you may overallocate—even if it contradicts your actual beliefs. This is not simply herd behaviour. It's identity-protection. We want to belong. And money, especially in public or semi-public forums, becomes a way of signalling identity: competent, savvy, successful, informed.

The risk is that performance becomes performative. You start investing not based on your goals or research, but based on what will look good to others—or feel good in conversation. The antidote is deeper self-definition. *Clarity about who you are and what you want defends you from mimetic drift.* You're less likely to be pulled into speculative trends if you're anchored by personal convictions. You're less likely to make erratic changes if your plan is built on reflection, not imitation.

This is not to suggest that identity should remain static. In fact, one of the most powerful effects of investing is that it *shapes* your self-concept over time. A person who begins investing with hesitation and anxiety often finds, after a few years of disciplined behaviour, that they've grown more patient, more analytical, more confident. The feedback loop is real. Repeated exposure to decision-making under uncertainty *trains judgement*. Repeated wins and recoveries *build self-trust*. Investing is not just about building wealth—it's about *building a temperament*.

That temperament includes more than rationality. It includes emotional range, cognitive flexibility, and moral clarity. The decisions you make about where to put your money are, inescapably, reflections of what you believe. Do you fund fossil fuels or renewables? Defence contractors or health-tech startups? Emerging markets or domestic infrastructure? These choices are not ethically neutral. And while some investors avoid these questions under the guise of pragmatism, the truth is: *your capital has impact, whether you acknowledge it or not.*

This is where values-based investing comes into sharper view—not as a branding exercise, but as a process of ethical coherence. You cannot claim to care about climate resilience while funding industries that profit from degradation. You cannot say you prioritise human rights while supporting companies with exploitative supply chains. This isn't about virtue signalling. It's about *alignment.* When your investments are aligned with your values, the psychological burden of contradiction is lifted. And when values are ignored, that burden compounds quietly—through discomfort, rationalisation, or disconnection.

That's why self-knowledge in investing is not a philosophical luxury. It is a practical necessity. The more self-aware you are, the more resilient your strategy becomes. Because eventually, every investor faces a test: a major loss, a market shock, a choice between staying the course or deviating under pressure. If you haven't built your portfolio in dialogue with your identity, you'll default to panic or imitation. But if your investing is an extension of your values, risk profile, and long-term intent, you can weather storms with greater clarity.

To cultivate that self-awareness, consider implementing a regular practice of reflection. After each significant investing decision—buy, sell, hold—pause and write down: *What did I feel before, during, and after? What story was I telling myself? What was I trying to protect or achieve?* Over time, these notes create a psychological map. They reveal your patterns—not just what you invest in, but *why* you act the way you do.

This map can become the most valuable asset in your toolkit. Because it evolves with you. As you gain experience, your fears change, your convictions deepen, and your patience strengthens. The process of becoming a better investor is, at its core, the process of becoming a clearer version of yourself.

You don't need to be a philosopher to invest with self-awareness. But you do need to *pay attention*—not just to markets, but to your own reactions. Not just to trends, but to your own time horizon. Not just to risk, but to your real appetite for it. Every chart you study, every headline you digest, every portfolio adjustment you make—all of it is filtered through you. *And that "you" is not fixed. It is learnable, observable, and shapeable.*

In the end, the best investors are not those who avoid mistakes entirely. They are the ones who use their mistakes as mirrors. Who review their emotional history with the same seriousness as their performance metrics. Who understand that the real edge is not just informational—it's psychological. It's having the courage to look inward, to ask hard questions, and to build a practice that reflects not just market conditions, but *who you are becoming.*

Values-Based Investing Without the Buzzwords:

For many investors, the moment they hear "values-based investing" or "ESG", their attention wavers—not because they don't care about impact or ethics, but because these terms have been diluted by marketing, bureaucracy, and ambiguity. They've become badges rather than behaviours. Acronyms without clarity. Labels that companies slap onto funds to appear conscientious, often with little underlying change in how capital is allocated. But beneath the noise lies a serious and timely question: *How do you ensure your investments reflect your principles—not just your profit targets?*

At its core, values-based investing isn't a separate category of investing—it's a way of thinking. It's the recognition that capital is never neutral. Every share purchased is a signal. Every asset allocation decision is a form of alignment—or misalignment—with the world you claim to want to live in. The question is not whether investing has impact. It always does. The real question is whether that impact is *intentional.*

Intentionality begins with specificity. General ethical sentiment—wanting to "do good"—rarely translates into coherent strategy. Vague preferences leave room for rationalisation. One might say they care about the environment while holding shares in multinational oil firms because "they're transitioning." Another might support human rights but invest in retailers with opaque supply chains due to performance metrics. The issue is not hypocrisy; it's lack of definition. *You can't align with your values until you define them operationally.*

Start with a clear articulation of your non-negotiables. Not what looks ethical on paper—but what you, based on your principles, believe should or should not be supported with capital. This may include exclusions (e.g. no tobacco, no weapons manufacturing, no surveillance tech) or affirmative themes (e.g. renewable energy, inclusive financial services, climate-resilient infrastructure). These are not checkboxes. They are philosophical commitments that require self-awareness and trade-off clarity. *Every value costs something. The question is whether it's worth it to you.*

The financial industry has responded to rising demand for ethical investing by offering ESG (Environmental, Social, and Governance) funds. In theory, ESG integrates non-financial factors into investment decisions to improve long-term outcomes and reduce risk. In practice, ESG has been implemented inconsistently, often with unclear methodologies and limited accountability. Some funds labelled as "sustainable" still hold fossil fuel giants. Others focus heavily on governance metrics while neglecting environmental impact altogether. The result is a market saturated with ESG products that vary wildly in rigour and intent.

This is why *due diligence is not optional.* If you want your investments to reflect your ethics, you cannot outsource your thinking to labels. Review fund prospectuses. Examine holdings. Study engagement strategies. Are they actively pushing companies toward better practices, or merely filtering based on public data? Are their metrics backward-looking or genuinely strategic? What does their stewardship record say about their convictions?

Being a values-based investor also means accepting complexity. There are few perfect companies. A solar energy firm may have strong environmental credentials but poor labour standards in its supply chain. A fintech platform serving underbanked communities may rely on aggressive data monetisation practices. Real-world ethical decisions are rarely binary. They require prioritisation. What values take precedence? What compromises are acceptable? What is your margin of ethical tolerance?

This is not paralysis—it's discernment. Ethical investing isn't about moral purity; it's about *consistency with intent*. If you are clear about what you stand for, then you are better equipped to evaluate which investments come close enough—and which fall too far short.

One powerful strategy is to shift from *exclusionary* models (avoiding harm) to *inclusionary* models (amplifying good). Instead of only asking, "What should I not invest in?" ask: *Where can my capital make the most constructive difference?* This reframing opens doors to investments in innovation: clean energy startups, social housing REITs, water infrastructure bonds, precision agriculture, or women-led enterprises in emerging markets. Many of these opportunities are unlisted or less liquid, requiring more work—but also offering more meaning.

Values-based investing also requires a long-term mindset. Ethical shifts do not manifest quarterly. Progress is often slow, non-linear, and contested. A company may begin carbon transition initiatives that show no immediate impact on earnings. A B Corp may choose to retain staff through economic downturns, dampening short-term profitability. If your ethical thesis rests on long-term societal benefit, you must calibrate your expectations accordingly. *Impatience is incompatible with true values alignment.*

Some critics argue that prioritising ethics over pure financial optimisation violates fiduciary responsibility. But this assumes that environmental or social considerations are divorced from risk. In reality, climate disruption, supply chain fragility, geopolitical instability, and regulatory shifts all have material implications for future cash flows. Values and valuation are not opposites. They are *interdependent*. Over time, firms that ignore sustainability may become uninvestable—not because of ideology, but because of structural obsolescence.

This doesn't mean that every values-aligned investment will outperform traditional benchmarks. There will be periods when extractive industries outperform regenerative ones. There will be times when high-ESG companies lag in growth. Values-based investing does not guarantee superior returns—it demands *return integrity*. That is, the capacity to look at your portfolio and say, "I made money in a way I can defend—not just strategically, but ethically."

This is why self-awareness is foundational. Two investors can both prioritise climate, yet differ meaningfully: one may pursue decarbonisation through green bonds and solar ETFs; the other might favour activist equity positions in legacy energy firms. Both are legitimate—provided they stem from thought, not trend. *There is no one-size-fits-all values-based portfolio. There is only coherence between belief and behaviour.*

Values-based investing also invites deeper questions about identity. What kind of investor do you want to be remembered as? What role does your capital play in the world beyond returns? Are you willing to forgo marginal gains to fund things that matter to you—or not? These are personal decisions. But they are also *civic* decisions. Because capital flows shape the incentives of the real economy. When you withhold investment from exploitative systems—or direct it towards regenerative ones—you're voting with more than your opinion. You're voting with your resources.

That said, values-based investing is not confined to public equities. It can be practised across asset classes: community lending, cooperative funds, venture capital, microfinance, and more. Many of these paths fall outside the default brokerage account and require more initiative. But they also offer a deeper sense of ownership. You are no longer just a market participant—you are a stakeholder in societal direction.

Even within traditional portfolios, you can apply ethical screens and proxy voting. If you use fund managers or advisors, ask them specific questions: *How do you incorporate sustainability into your research process? What are your active ownership strategies? How do you respond when portfolio companies violate core principles?* Your questions shape industry standards. When enough investors demand substance over marketing, the system evolves.

It's worth noting that values-based investing is not only for the affluent. Even modest portfolios can express meaningful alignment. The key is not how much you invest—but *how thoughtfully* you invest. Your portfolio should be a reflection of what you know, what you believe, and what you are willing to stand behind. This is as much a moral stance as a financial one.

At its most developed, values-based investing is not a label. It is a practice. A habit of questioning. A refusal to let convenience override conscience. And a belief that the purpose of capital is not just to grow—but to *serve something beyond itself*. The market rewards efficiency. But you get to define what that efficiency is in service of.

Ultimately, values-based investing is not a trend. It is a test of clarity. And the test is not whether your portfolio is perfect, but whether it is *honest*. Whether it reflects who you are—not just as an investor, but as a participant in the world you're helping to shape.

Legacy Thinking for First-Time Investors:

Most first-time investors begin with personal goals in mind—retirement, home ownership, financial independence, perhaps even generational wealth. These are all valid and deeply motivating. But few pause early on to consider the broader arc: *What will my investing habits leave behind—not just in wealth, but in wisdom?* Legacy is not something reserved for philanthropists, tycoons, or family offices. Legacy is built in micro-decisions, in financial habits, in the way values compound alongside capital.

Thinking in terms of legacy challenges a short-term mindset. It invites a shift from accumulation to stewardship. Accumulation asks, *What can I build for myself?* Stewardship asks, *What am I responsible for preserving, improving, or transmitting—whether to future family members, institutions, or causes I care about?* For first-time investors, this might sound like a problem for another decade. But delaying legacy thinking postpones the clarity it can offer right now. *You do not need to be wealthy to leave a legacy—you need to be intentional.*

The first and most overlooked pillar of legacy is *financial literacy*. It is not the size of your portfolio that shapes what your children or mentees inherit—it's whether they know how to use it wisely. Studies have consistently shown that inherited wealth without financial education tends to deplete within two to three generations. Assets passed down without context become burdens, not blessings. By contrast, modest investments accompanied by clear principles, stories, and instructions often carry disproportionate value.

So what does it mean to pass on financial wisdom? It begins with transparency. Too many families treat investing as a private or taboo subject—until crisis forces a rushed disclosure. This secrecy leaves younger generations vulnerable to confusion, conflict, or poor decisions when wealth eventually changes hands. A legacy-minded investor creates a culture of shared understanding long before it's necessary. They document their investment philosophy. They talk openly about risk tolerance, ethical preferences, decision-making frameworks, and even past mistakes. *They leave a map, not just a vault.*

Legacy thinking also challenges the idea that personal success is an isolated victory. Every investor is a beneficiary of compounding forces that came before: stable institutions, financial innovation, often family support or inherited knowledge. Paying that forward—whether through mentorship, education, or structurally inclusive investing—is not an act of charity. It is a form of justice. It acknowledges that wealth is rarely self-made in the strictest sense. *The long-term investor who integrates this view builds not just a portfolio, but a philosophy of intergenerational responsibility.*

Take, for example, the growing interest in custodial accounts, junior ISAs, or family investment trusts—not simply as tax-advantaged tools, but as teaching instruments. When used with intentionality, these vehicles become opportunities for hands-on education. A parent might let a child help choose one ETF to include. A grandparent might write a short note each year explaining why they favour dividend growth over speculation. A guardian might set conditions for distributions based on educational or entrepreneurial milestones. *These small acts frame wealth as a tool tied to behaviour, not entitlement.*

But legacy thinking isn't just about family. It also asks: *What footprint do my investments leave on society?* This invites a deeper look at how your capital shapes the economy, policy, innovation, and the environment. Do you want your legacy to include having funded extractive industries—or having accelerated sustainable solutions? Do you want to be remembered as an investor who prioritised convenience, or one who insisted on alignment between money and meaning? These are not moralistic questions—they are strategic. *The future you help capitalise is the one you and your successors will live in.*

For institutional thinkers and thoughtful professionals, this dimension of legacy might express itself through donor-advised funds, impact investing, or social enterprises. For others, it might simply mean choosing pension funds that don't underwrite industries at odds with their values. Either way, *legacy is less about magnitude, more about intent.* What story does your portfolio tell when you're no longer there to explain it?

Another underappreciated aspect of legacy is *behavioural modelling.* What others observe in your financial conduct often outlasts what you explicitly teach. Do you panic during market volatility, or do you stay the course with discipline? Do you chase fads, or follow a clearly defined strategy? Do you discuss money with shame or with equanimity? These patterns form part of the behavioural inheritance passed down—often unconsciously. If a child watches you regularly rebalance your portfolio according to a thought-out plan, they're more likely to internalise composure as a default posture. *You're not just investing for them. You're showing them how to think.*

And what about those with no direct heirs? Legacy can be institutional. One can support financial education programmes, fund scholarships, endow research, or write publicly about personal investing lessons. Some of the most lasting legacies are intellectual, not financial. Benjamin Graham's impact on investing dwarfs the value of any one fund. So does John Bogle's creation of index funds. Their legacies were built on insight, clarity, and accessibility—not family dynasties. *You don't need lineage to leave a legacy. You need perspective.*

This brings us to a crucial psychological pivot: legacy thinking softens the grip of ego. It helps reframe investment success away from personal scoreboard metrics and towards enduring contribution. It tamps down the temptation to over-optimise every decision in pursuit of a perfect return. The investor who thinks in decades—not just for themselves, but for others—begins to ask questions like: *Is this investment defensible in the light of my values? Would I want this holding to be part of the story people remember? What am I normalising with this allocation?* These are questions of maturity, not just of finance.

Moreover, legacy thinking affects *how* you invest—your asset allocation, your holding period, your choice of partners. If you're building with an eye toward durability, you may favour instruments with resilience over flash. You may look at dividends as more than income—they become reinvestable lessons in patience. You may see tax planning not as a loophole exercise, but as a way to ensure the continuity of contribution. *Everything begins to bend toward longevity.*

Critically, legacy also includes planning for succession. It's not enough to hope someone will manage your portfolio wisely after you're gone. A responsible investor outlines contingencies: who will manage the assets, where the key documents are located, how trusts or estates are structured, what your intentions were behind certain investments. The absence of such planning can destroy years of thoughtful work in a matter of months. *A good legacy is portable. It survives your absence because it was built with transfer in mind.*

Lastly, there's a philosophical dimension to legacy that no spreadsheet can capture. At some point, every thoughtful investor confronts the question: *How much is enough?* Legacy thinking requires a reckoning with this boundary. If there is no definition of "enough," accumulation becomes an open loop—ceaseless, restless, untethered from purpose. But if you can define "enough," you create space for generosity, for mentorship, for teaching, for sharing. *The moment you no longer need more is the moment you can most powerfully offer guidance.*

In this sense, legacy is not something to tack on once you've reached wealth. It is something you practise throughout the investment process. In your clarity of strategy. In your ethical stance. In your communication with others. In your curiosity to learn and share. It doesn't require a title, or an inheritance, or even perfect foresight. It requires only a commitment to invest with others in mind—and a willingness to make your thinking part of what you leave behind.

When Enough Is Enough:

Modern investing culture, fuelled by performance charts, social comparison, and an endless stream of financial media, has a peculiar blind spot: it rarely asks what the money is for. Accumulation becomes the objective by default. Benchmarks are external, not internal—beating the index, reaching seven figures, retiring a decade early. But when you strip away the marketing, the algorithms, and the noise, a far more essential question emerges: *What is enough—for you?* Without a personal definition of "enough," investing risks becoming a treadmill without a destination. You run faster but feel no closer to satisfaction.

The notion of "enough" isn't a constraint. It's a liberating boundary. It offers a framework for agency, a filter through which you can assess opportunity, risk, and trade-offs. When you know what enough looks like—not just financially, but psychologically—you reclaim investing as a tool rather than a scoreboard. Without it, you are perpetually vulnerable to FOMO, mission drift, and optimisation spirals that often lead to burnout rather than prosperity.

Consider the practical implications of never defining enough. Your investment strategy becomes reactive. If markets are up, you wish you had invested more aggressively. If they're down, you regret not being more conservative. Your time horizon extends arbitrarily—because you never built a terminal point into the plan. You may overwork, overanalyse, overcommit capital to strategies you don't understand, or chase returns in spaces misaligned with your temperament. *Without enough, you pursue more—without clarity, purpose, or peace.*

Warren Buffett, despite his extreme wealth, lives in the same Omaha house he bought in 1958. That's not frugality theatre; it's a signal. He has long understood that lifestyle creep does not correlate linearly with satisfaction. And he has been open about his view that beyond a certain point, more money adds utility only at the margins. Research in behavioural economics reinforces this. Studies consistently show that past a modest threshold—enough to cover comfort, security, and discretionary joy—additional wealth contributes far less to well-being than time autonomy, social connection, or meaningful work.

For the thoughtful investor, the question becomes: *How do I define enough—not abstractly, but in numbers, values, and actions?* This is not about minimalist virtue-signalling. It's about designing a life and portfolio with intention. Enough may include a debt-free home, sufficient passive income to cover basic expenses, a buffer for medical emergencies, and funds for intergenerational support or travel. But the shape of that number must be personal. It must reflect your cost of living, your tolerance for risk, your vision for contribution. Importantly, it should also reflect your time preference: how much future you are willing to delay in order to maximise a future self you may never meet.

This requires self-honesty. Are you building wealth to impress peers, or to create options? Are you accumulating because you genuinely need more security, or because you haven't paused to reflect on the sufficiency of what you've already built? These are not trivial distinctions. They govern the levers you pull—the leverage you use, the volatility you tolerate, the lifestyle you adopt, the psychological burden you carry.

The financial industry is not built to help you define enough. It is built to grow assets under management. It monetises your dissatisfaction, your uncertainty, your aspiration for more. Platforms profit from churn. Advisors earn more when your definition of success inflates with your portfolio. Most content encourages movement, not stillness; hunger, not contentment. That's why anchoring yourself in your own values is an act of rebellion—and of deep strategic clarity. *Knowing what is enough inoculates you from manipulation.*

Let's take this further. Enough doesn't mean static. It means defined *at intervals*. What was enough at 30 may not be enough at 50. Life stage, health, dependants, inflation, and changing priorities all influence the shape of sufficiency. But the process of redefining it—deliberately, periodically—is what matters. It ensures that you're not drifting. That you're not investing by default but by design.

One effective tool is the personal financial mission statement. This is not about asset allocation or retirement targets. It's a short document—sometimes just a paragraph—that articulates your aims: *Why are you investing? What matters more to you than returns? What trade-offs are you unwilling to make? What will you do when the goal is met?* This living statement can act as a compass in volatile times. It also becomes a deeply clarifying document to share with family or future inheritors of your wealth.

Consider this example: a first-generation investor in their mid-30s sets a goal to accumulate £1 million in investable assets by age 50, with the intent to semi-retire and work part-time on mission-driven projects. They arrive at that figure not because it looks impressive, but because it's rooted in projected living expenses, risk buffers, and values. Once that goal is in sight, they begin shifting their portfolio to lower-volatility assets. They reduce equity exposure, not out of fear, but from design. They resist the urge to chase higher returns when they're already financially secure—because their goal was freedom, not outperformance. *This is what it looks like to let enough guide behaviour, not just philosophy.*

Defining enough also recalibrates your relationship with volatility. Investors with no defined end point see drawdowns as existential. But when your plan is anchored in sufficiency, not excess, you can absorb short-term shocks with greater equanimity. If your lifestyle doesn't require perpetual outperformance, your investing choices gain flexibility. You can take breaks from monitoring markets. You can rebalance with conviction rather than anxiety. You stop overcorrecting at every headline. *Enough is a stabiliser—not just financially, but emotionally.*

There's a humility embedded in enough that also protects against hubris. You stop believing in your own infallibility. You acknowledge that more is not always better, and that beyond a point, marginal gains come with increasing complexity, risk, and opportunity cost. Instead of stacking leverage, you build robustness.

Instead of idolising liquidity, you prioritise longevity. These trade-offs aren't defensive—they're mature. They reflect a shift from maximisation to sustainability.

Enough also creates space for generosity. When you know you have what you need, you can afford to help others without resentment. Whether that's donating to causes, mentoring others, or supporting family, the act of giving becomes rooted in confidence rather than performance anxiety. Some of the most effective philanthropists, educators, and community builders are those who stopped chasing more and started deploying what they had with focused intent.

There's a final, more existential reason to define enough: it helps you exit gracefully. One of the great tragedies in investing is the inability to stop. To not just keep going, but to keep escalating risk, workload, and pressure—long after it's necessary. Markets are full of stories of individuals who doubled their net worth, then halved it by refusing to adjust once "enough" had been reached. Whether it's a retiree who stayed overexposed to tech stocks, or a fund manager who took one trade too many, the cautionary tales all echo the same lesson: *without a stopping rule, success becomes fragile.*

Ultimately, "enough" is not a number. It's a philosophy. It is the rare ability to look at your financial life and say, *this satisfies the needs I've defined, not the insecurities I've inherited.* It doesn't require withdrawal from ambition. It requires upgrading your ambition—to include peace of mind, ethical clarity, and time to live in accordance with your own values. The investor who knows when enough is enough is not settling. They're arriving.

Conclusion
You're Not Just an Investor. You're a Builder of Time:

To invest is to assert order against the whirl of uncertainty. It is a quiet declaration that the future merits attention, that your judgement carries weight, and that time can be shaped rather than merely endured. Beneath the tickers, graphs, and relentless headlines lies a deeper truth: each financial decision is also a philosophical one. Investing deliberately is not merely about allocating capital—it is an exercise in agency.

This work has never promised shortcuts, perfect market timing, or the ability to predict macro pivots with uncanny precision. Its aim has been subtler: to offer a framework for seeing clearly, one that honours both the mathematical power of compounding and the human element that so often derails it. A system that values resilience over reflex, reflection over replication, and clarity over noise. If it has succeeded, what you carry forward is not a rigid formula but a fortified sense of sovereignty over your choices.

Today's investor confronts a barrage of distractions: the flicker of daily prices, the siren call of trending tickers, the dopamine loops of news cycles masquerading as insight. Yet the most crucial capital under management is rarely financial. It is attentional, emotional, temporal. The finest investing transforms attention into intention. One is extractive; the other, creative. One makes you chase. The other makes you construct.

To construct is to shape time, tangibly, deliberately, and consistently. A disciplined, diversified portfolio is more than market participation; it is a manifestation of values extended across decades. You are building something that safeguards your family, funds your ambitions, expresses your worldview, and may well outlast you. Compound interest is a fact; compounding conviction is an achievement.

Most approach investing with a single, often misleading question: how do I beat the market? A more potent inquiry asks: how do I stop the market from beating me? How do I resist provocation, remain steady amid extremes, and respond to a 15 per cent overnight drop with clarity rather than panic? The accomplished investor is not the one winning every trade but the one who knows when not to trade, which signals merit attention, and, above all, who understands themselves.

If investing is a mirror, it shows biases for immediacy, unease with uncertainty, a craving for approval, tendencies to under- or overreact, or to defer responsibility. This is feedback, not failure. Feedback is rare currency in the market; it is an edge, provided you have the courage to listen.

Many books close with prescriptive rules, templates, or allocation guides. But these tools are only effective once the internal work is done. Without clarity about what you are building, without defining enough, without understanding the role of money in your life, such tools become instruments of distraction. You tinker instead of growing, chase instead of planting. You react in a game that rewards patience.

This chapter is not a curtain call—it is a prompt to return to first principles. The initial act—opening this book, committing to serious thought about investing—was an act of belief: in your time, in the power to shape the future, in your agency within an imperfect system. That belief now requires safeguarding. Cynicism is easy. It dresses surrender in sophistication. Vision is harder: sober, deliberate recognition that your choices matter, that intentional allocation of capital can support autonomy, impact, and identity.

Discipline here is not grit alone but design: the intentional creation of structures, signals, and systems that keep you aligned when emotion tempts deviation. One of the most radical acts is to think in decades—not because long timeframes guarantee returns, but because they alter your questions, shift perspective from reactive to proactive, and distinguish signal from noise. It is the mental pivot from participating in markets to owning your space within them.

Markets will evolve. Assets will rotate. Politics and crises will inject volatility. Yet your role remains stable: you are a steward—not only of capital but of attention, time, and trust. You are the architect of the rules you follow, the beliefs you revise, the strategies you implement, and the legacy—financial and intellectual—you leave behind.

If this chapter offers a final invitation, it is to resist default thought, passive consumption, and the notion that investing is reserved for insiders. You are not a spectator. You are not merely participating. You are constructing time. Each decision, each pound invested, each moment of restraint, designs the future you will inhabit. And a future that is sustainable, meaningful, and aligned with your values will not arise by accident. It will be built by one who chooses belief over cynicism, strategy over reaction, and agency over inertia.

That someone is now you.

The journey ends with a return to the book's core idea:

Investing, despite its charts, algorithms, and earnings calls, is ultimately a declaration of belief. Not blind belief in a particular stock or fund, but belief in the very possibility that the future can be shaped by intentional action. That your decisions today, however small, carry weight beyond the present. To invest is to stand at the intersection of uncertainty and conviction and to say, *I will act anyway.* It is this posture—rooted in agency—that underpins the philosophy of this book.

The dominant narratives around investing are often framed in the language of competition: beat the market, outsmart the crowd, capture alpha. But this framing is flawed at its foundation. It assumes that the market is something to be conquered, rather than understood. It frames success as a matter of domination, rather than alignment. It prizes aggression over awareness. And in doing so, it subtly removes you—the investor—from the equation. You become a technician, a spectator of volatility, a reactor to trends. You outsource not just strategy, but self-direction.

The premise here is different. This is not a book about optimisation for its own sake. It is not a playbook for traders or a hedge fund's manual in disguise. It is a book about agency—about reclaiming your capacity to choose thoughtfully, consistently, and with integrity in an environment designed to provoke reactivity. Markets reward the patient, the grounded, and the adaptive. But they first test whether you've earned those qualities through self-awareness.

The moment you put money into the market, you reveal what you believe about the world. That growth is possible. That progress is probabilistic but real. That innovation matters. That time, more than timing, is your greatest ally. Investing is not just a financial act—it is a philosophical stance. And like any philosophy, it becomes meaningful only when internalised and enacted.

This is why the most essential question in investing is not *What should I buy?* but *What do I believe?* Your asset allocation, your risk tolerance, your holding periods—they all flow downstream of that core. If you do not know what you believe about risk, time, uncertainty, or purpose, then markets will define it for you. And when the market dictates your behaviour, it becomes not a tool, but a master.

Cynicism poses as sophistication in investing. The detached shrug, the mocking of "retail investors," the obsession with short-term moves, the relentless search for inefficiencies to exploit—all of this can feel like knowledge. But cynicism is the easiest intellectual posture. It requires no work, no courage, no commitment. It is reactive by nature and parasitic in effect. Belief, by contrast, is active. It requires you to take a position, to stake your time and resources on a vision of the world that may not yet exist. *To invest with belief is to accept that your values have relevance even under uncertainty.*

One of the most radical things you can do in modern markets is to be intentional. Not merely tactical, but values-driven. This does not mean putting every pound into impact funds or divesting from every controversial sector. It means knowing *why* you hold what you hold. It means aligning your financial behaviour with your intellectual framework, not someone else's forecast. It means treating your portfolio not just as a collection of securities, but as an externalisation of internal clarity.

This is why the best investors aren't always the most educated, or the most informed, or the most mathematically gifted. They are the ones who have learned to live in harmony with both the market and themselves. They do not panic when volatility strikes because they have already rehearsed the emotional terrain. They do not sell in manias or buy in collapses because their strategy is not dictated by headlines. *They understand that investing is not just what you do with your money—it is what you do with your mind.*

Living in harmony with the market does not mean blind faith in its fairness or function. It means acknowledging its complexity without being consumed by it. It means respecting its unpredictability while still participating in its growth. It means operating within it without being absorbed by its rhythms. Harmony is not passivity—it is posture. It is how you stand when things sway.

And that posture is cultivated—not gifted. It is trained over time through observation, reflection, and deliberate practice. Through rebalancing not in panic, but by design. Through resisting the itch to overtrade. Through setting long-term parameters and revisiting them only when your beliefs—not the market—have changed. *This is not behaviour management; it is identity management.*

When you understand investing as an act of agency, everything changes. Risk becomes not something to eliminate, but to calibrate. Diversification becomes not a buzzword, but a statement of humility. Rebalancing becomes not an intervention, but a form of stewardship. These are not tactics—they are expressions of perspective. And perspective is what you must protect above all else, especially when the market tries to shake it loose.

You will not beat the market over every quarter. Nor should you try. But you can live above the market's noise. You can learn to measure success not by short-term outperformance but by the quality of your decisions relative to your values. You can treat volatility not as a threat, but as a reminder to return to principle. *This is how you stop playing the market's game and start playing your own.*

To do this well requires accepting a paradox. You must act with both conviction and humility. Conviction to hold firm when your thesis is sound but tested. Humility to revise your thinking when new evidence emerges. The art is not picking sides—it is learning to live within that tension. This is the work of a mature investor. Not to predict, but to prepare. Not to react, but to reflect. Not to dominate, but to adapt.

And adaptation requires honesty. Not just about markets, but about yourself. About what you're actually trying to build. About when enough is enough. About how much risk you're truly willing to bear. About whether your current behaviour matches your stated goals. Self-deception is more dangerous than any bear market, because it corrodes from within. A clear-eyed investor is a rare thing. But they are also, not coincidentally, a durable one.

This book has argued that the most overlooked edge in investing is psychological sovereignty. Not independence in the shallow sense of doing the opposite of everyone else, but independence in the deeper sense: knowing *why* you act when you act. Markets cannot be controlled. But your interface with them can be. And once you see that, you are no longer just participating—you are creating. Not out of hubris, but out of integrity.

That integrity must be renewed. Investing is not a one-time act of clarity; it is a repeated commitment to it. It is a discipline of return—to principle, to reflection, to your own definition of success. Agency is not granted once; it is exercised continually. Every trade, every holding, every review is a chance to say: *this is what I believe, and this is how I'll show it.*

If there is a closing message here, it is not to be more confident, or more clever, or even more informed. It is to be more *deliberate*. The market is not asking you to have perfect timing or total certainty. It is asking whether you are willing to stand still while others sprint, to think while others shout, to plant while others harvest. In short, it is asking whether you can hold your own mind when others offer you theirs.

That is agency. That is harmony. That is investing—not as performance, but as practice. Not as conquest, but as composition. Not as chasing alpha, but as building time.

About the Author

Julian Crest writes at the intersection of money and meaning. After years of observing how first-time investors stumble—not for lack of intelligence, but for lack of perspective—he began crafting guides that help people build wealth through clarity, not complexity. His work blends financial insight with philosophical depth, inviting readers to rethink investing not just as a tool, but as a practice of personal agency. Julian's mission is to help people invest in alignment with who they are and the lives they want to live. He believes that ownership isn't just about stocks—it's about becoming the kind of person who moves through uncertainty with intention.

www.ingramcontent.com/pod-product-compliance
Lightning Source LLC
Chambersburg PA
CBHW031348230926
51848CB00002B/441